No More Bondage

Breaking Free From the Prison of Generational Sins!

By Pamela Sauer

Xulon PRESS

First, I want to thank the Lord for setting me free from the generational sins that have haunted my family for years!

To my husband, Randy, and my children, Amanda, Ashley, Andrew, and Alison, I thank you for your love and support as I wrote this book.

To Carole Liston, I would like to thank you for your hours of tedious editing! You never gave up on me!
Thank you for your constant encouragement and belief that I had a story that needed to be told!
I could not have done it without you!

To Tracy Culbertson, thank you for all your help.

To my sister, Karen, thanks for praying and believing in me!
I love all of you!

Jesus looked at them and said,
"With man this is impossible,
but with God all things are possible."

Matthew 19:26 (NIV)

Have you been held captive? This book is written to all those who have been in some form of prison, whether mental or physical. This is the story of how I found myself in the "Prison of Despair" and the journey the Lord Jesus Christ took me on to set me free! I pray this book leads you into a closer relationship with the only One who can rid us from the bondage of the past!

In my anguish I cried to the LORD,
and he answered by setting me free.

Psalm 118:5 (NIV)

Freedom From the Prison of Despair

I sit and wonder: "Why am I here?"
Please make this mess disappear.
Arguing and alcohol, couriers of despair,
Deposit their burdens, more than I can bear.

Anguished mother hurts me,
Father runs and flees,
Bitterness consumes the heart,
Alone and scared, I want to part.

Drugs ease the pain away,
Isn't that what some say?
I find that this cannot be so.
My heart is still so full of woe.

Dark prison surrounded by disdain,
No release from these chains,
Anger internalized, must rebel,
No escape from this hell.

Will anyone hear the plea?
What is the key?
Will I make it through?
What am I to do?

Jesus, rescue me!
And the scattered debris,
Hurt and pain is all I know,
Let the healing powers flow.

Jesus, please come near,
And wash away the tears
Despair must depart
Once hope fills the heart!

I felt His presence right away—
He began the work that very day
Healing came slowly, over time
Nevertheless, healing was mine.

Chains off, indeed I'm free—
No more bondage for me!
Generational sins came to an end
Now my heart is on the mend!

Pamela Sauer 4/4/06

Table of Contents

CHAPTER ONE

The Foundation for My Prison

⟡

They have greatly oppressed me from my youth,
but they have not gained the victory over me.
Plowmen have plowed my back and made their furrows
long. But the LORD is righteous; He has cut me free
from the cords of the wicked.
Psalm 129:2-4 (NIV)

It was late in the day, around dinnertime. The sun was beginning to set. The neighborhood kids and I were playing touch football on the school playground across from my home. Since I was the youngest, my job was to hike the ball. Everyone was caught up in the game, laughing and carrying on. Then all of a sudden, everything halted, and silence filled the air. The only noise was the sound of a car in the distance. Everyone's attention turned and watched the events that were about to unfold. A police car came barreling down the road and stopped abruptly at my house. Two police officers got out of the car and rushed into my home. My mind filled with confusion as I anxiously watched and waited. Then as I gazed at my house, the screen door flew open and my father came out with his hands behind him. The police followed. Handcuffed, my father was ushered by the police into the back seat of the patrol car. I was so embarrassed, and my head immediately fell down. Instantly, shame covered me like a blanket. None of my friends said a word to me, and I did not dare say anything to them. My feet began to move as if they were on their own, and before I knew it, I was at the front door of my house. I leapt into the house, frantically searching for my mother. Breathless, I asked her, "Why was Dad arrested? What did he do?"

My mother shouted back with tears rolling down her face, "We had a fight; your father was drunk again! He threw the iron at me and so I called the police."

After this episode, I felt as though my life was a ship on the tossing sea, destined for nowhere. The elements were in control and I was not. The sea of despair was constantly moving the ship. Sometimes the storms could be frightening, and I would pray for calmer waters to return. When the storm cleared, security was not to be found, because the waters were always stirring, just as if I were a small boat in the sea, and at any moment another storm could be brewing on the horizon. This anticipation of the next storm brewing was something I carried daily. My insecurities were deepening into an abyss, and my heart was sinking. I was in a mental prison cell where anger was becoming my friend.

Within twenty-four hours my father was home again. Nothing about the prior incident was ever mentioned. I internalized my anger; there was no one to verbalize my feelings to. I was not to bring it up; avoidance was the standard behavior in my house. I loved my parents, but communication was so closed and being so young, it was impossible for me to understand what our difficulties were. Why couldn't my parents be like "normal" people, I wondered. I was in a state of frustration!

* * *

Now for a little background on my family: my father was a very problematic man; he struggled with alcoholism all of his life, and on top of that he was a very strict disciplinarian. To put it bluntly, he was unstable, which led him to live a life like a revolving door, in and out of his children's lives, moving from place to place. Since he did not talk a lot about his past, it is difficult to say just how many demons he fought. I believe my father's insecurities played a huge role in his behavior. It seemed as though he was suspiciously protective and wanted to control everyone and everything around him. This was taken to the extreme with the four older children. My father never allowed my siblings to participate in any sports, nor did he allow many friends around the house. He seemed to think that if he had been robbed of his childhood, then they should be robbed of theirs! Because of his tyranny, two of my sisters quit school and married around the age of fifteen. Home held too much turmoil for them. Needless to say, our home was not a haven; rather it was a prison run by a dreadful warden.

However, this dysfunction came from both sides of my family. My mother was from the hills of Arkansas and had grown up in abject poverty. Her family lived in a little frame house, surrounded by the forest and heated solely by a wood stove. In the kitchen there was a pump for the faucet. This little wooden house consisted of a few rooms filled with many beds, which were covered by hand-made quilts for bedspreads. The house did have electricity, but that was the limit in terms of modern conveniences. The outhouse was about a hundred feet behind the house. A stranger would have labeled my mother's family as "hillbillies." My grandmother even chewed tobacco and wore dresses all the time, complete with tennis shoes! Her purse was her prized possession, which she guarded with her life. My grandfather was always wearing overalls, and he wore round wire-framed glasses, much like what President Truman wore. He had a glass eye and threatened to take it out and scare his grandchildren with it! My mother had several brothers and sisters. Just as my father had problems with alcohol, her father struggled with alcoholism, too. I do not know many details, but I am aware that my grandfather fondled her as a child. It is hard to say just what kind of life my mother led before marriage, but I am convinced it was wretched. She too was robbed of the normal, precious childhood memories that many people cherish. She must have looked for a way to escape, just as my sisters and I did.

When my father came into my mother's life, he came to town by means of a traveling carnival. He enchanted my mother. Imagine how exhilarating the smells, lights, and music of the carnival must have been to her! Here she was in her drab existence, and a handsome man who seemed so wise in the ways of the world, was interested in her. What a thrill for a young girl with plain looks and a melancholy personality! Not only was this man "worldly wise," but he had very distinct features: coal black hair, beautiful olive skin, and magnetic gray eyes! I can see how she would have fallen head over heels for him. I know she assumed he was her ticket out of her "pitiful life." She, being so young, certainly must have fantasized how she was about to escape her impoverished life in Arkansas. She was only fifteen with an eighth grade education, and the future was full of excitement. Her new life was beginning. Their union began in 1951. It would not be long until she would realize my father was not her knight in shining armor. My mother had been deceived. She had just married a good-looking charlatan. When these two were married, it was a certainty that their bondage would be bred into yet another generation. Immediately after their marriage, they began their family. The first four children were close in age. Because she was so young, my mother could handle the stresses of raising the first four children more easily than the last two. Then I came along six years later. I am the fifth in the birth order. It appears as though I came from a large family, but because of age variation we really did not grow up under one roof. We were a dispersed family, physically and mentally By the time my younger sister was born six years later, my mother had become very weary. Not only had she grown tired of my father's antics, but also her past began to disturb her. She was in her late thirties now, and like many women in that age range, she started dealing with her past. In those days, an incestuous relationship was shameful, as though it were the victim's fault. Not only was she wounded, but she also carried condemnation in her heart for violations that had been done to her that were beyond her control. Satan tormented her with the past.

Because of my mother's inner torment and my father's inconsistent behavior our lives were drastically affected. In fact, my memories of my youth are lost in a blur. There are but a few things I do call to mind. I recall we moved a lot, and I went from school to school. I remember going to first grade at Lincoln Elementary, and in those days school started around the first of September. My birthday happens to be the first of September. Mrs. Jamison was my first grade teacher. She was young and pretty, and she had dark hair and a warm smile. She had the kind of smile that speaks to you when you walk in a room, the kind that whispers, "I am your friend."

On the first day of school, Mrs. Jamison called me up to her desk and confided, "Pam, I know it is your birthday this week, and since you are so special, the school has decided to give you free lunches."

I truly believed I was special! I had no idea I was receiving free lunches because I was poor! Her kindness protected my dignity, and I will never forget her love and compassion. She was the quintessential first grade teacher. I enjoyed school that year. God revealed his love to me through Mrs. Jamison.

Another good memory I do have is of Christmas 1969. I very much wanted a doll named "Tippy Toes." Every time I saw a commercial advertising that doll, I would comment on how much I wanted it. Everyone in a one-mile radius was aware of what I expected from Santa that Christmas. This doll had curly blonde hair, big blue eyes, and dark eyelashes. She had rosy cheeks and creamy skin. She came with a tricycle that actually moved. She also was able to walk on her tippy toes, thus her name "Tippy Toes."

A very kind man lived across the street from us. His name was Paul Ketterman. I would go over and talk to him daily. He was always out working in his yard. We would discuss what I was learning at school. He listened so attentively. He made me feel as though I was his friend. Anyway, I must have mentioned how much I wanted that doll to him several times. The sweet man went out and purchased that doll for me. He also had compassion on my family, and he bought us a Christmas tree that year. When I woke up Christmas morning, I knew my prayers had been answered. Tippy Toes was my baby doll! This was the hand of the Lord at work in my life. This season was a joyful time, but it was not long before my father got restless once again.

We never stayed in one place very long, and we moved away from that kind neighbor, Mr. Ketterman. I had lost yet another friend. The next home we moved to came with a tetherball pole. I begged my parents for a tetherball. Miraculously they got me that tetherball! In my times of pain, I would go out and play tetherball for hours. It was just that ball and me, and I would hit it as hard as I could. The ball would go flying and then I would hit it again until that ball wrapped all the way around that pole. It was therapy for me. For the moment, my frustrations were released with every hit of the ball. This became my passion. At recess in school I would race outside and hog the tetherball. I became very good at this little sport, but like everything in the past this too would be taken from me.

Enjoyable times were few, but they did occur during my father's times of sobriety. During these moments of soberness, my parents were able to function as a "normal" couple. In fact, you would have found laughter in our home. Life seemed so different when my father was sober, employed, and in church. We were not wealthy by any means, but we had food on the table. However, these times only lasted for short intervals. Stability was not a permanent resident in our home.

Running was my father's way of life, and many times he took us along with him. From house to house we lived. We were never fortunate enough to own a home: we were able to only rent. I do not understand why, but my parents expected government assistance as though it was owed to them. Welfare became our means of life. They refused to realize it was my father's substance abuse that created many of their money problems. They always thought opportunities were closed to them. They would not face the harm sin caused in their lives or the lives of their children. They never took notice of why I was struggling in school. I would begin to settle in a school, and then we would move again and again.

By the time I was nine we had lived in so many different houses I cannot even begin to count them. My older siblings could not take any more of my parents' antics, and they left home. My family now consisted of my mother, my father, my little sister, and me. My father suddenly decided to move to Miami, Oklahoma. It was just forty-five minutes from my hometown. I really do not remember why we moved there. I guess because one of my sisters and my brother were living there at the time, or perhaps it was for employment. Whatever the reason, we moved and rented a little house in a small neighborhood. In my recollection, life was more in disarray than normal. Later, I would find out that my mother had an affair with a much younger man that lived next door to us. When my father became aware of this, he and my mother fought and he took off. Within a short time period of his leaving, probably a day or two, my mother finally broke. Her life of sin and despair took its toll. She lost all ability to function mentally and had a nervous breakdown. It was as though she could not cope with even the simplest of tasks. She was quickly committed to the nearest asylum.

By this time I was about ten years old and my little sister was four. We were taken to our older sister's house to live. My sister Karen was not too excited to have us there. She thought she had escaped mom and dad's turmoil through her marriage, and here we were in the middle of her home. Even though I was very young, I was aware that Tonda and I were not wanted. I cried out to God for help. Thank God, my father miraculously returned within days and took responsibility for us.

My father was too prideful to return to our former home. The next day we were on an adventure looking for a new house. One particular property stands out in my mind. It was decent from the outside. It was a little white house with a nice front porch made from pieces of stone and had probably been built in the 1930s. Nothing about the outside appearance would have given us a clue of what waited inside. As we walked up the porch stairs, I was excited about seeing the inside. With each move, I always anticipated which room would be mine. My father opened the door, and we walked in. Right away, my anticipation turned to weariness, as the house was not very neat. The living room was dirty, as though the former residents had left in a hurry. I stayed close to my father and followed him into the kitchen. As I stepped into this room, I heard a sickening crunch under my feet. I looked down and to my surprise, realized that I had just stepped on a cluster of roaches. I looked up on the kitchen counter and saw even more coming out the cabinets. Soon there were hundreds of roaches scurrying around. Even though it was the middle of the day, the roaches were moving as if it was dark and we had just flipped on the light. My father looked at me and asserted, "We need to get some pest control bombs and clean this place up so we can move in."

I could not believe he was serious. I was terrified. How desperate was he? He went out and bought a couple of the bombs. I watched him set them off. The next day we returned to that house, but even though the house was full of dead roaches, many had survived. The decision not to move in was made in a moment. We eventually found a new place and moved immediately. This was the way he lived his whole life. Always making decisions in an instant that affected everyone around him!

This began a very difficult season for us. What was happening with my mother was beyond my understanding. When we went to visit her in the asylum, it was just like a scene in the movie, *One Flew Over the Cuckoo's Nest*. She whispered eerie things to me, such as, "They are trying to kill me in this place," and, "They are mistreating me here. They won't give me any sanitary napkins."

This was discomforting for a little ten-year-old girl to assimilate, and it literally gave me nightmares. I hated to visit her. That asylum was filled with oppression and depression. The evil spirits were lurking around furiously in that place. This made me feel so insecure that it became traumatizing for me to spend the night with a friend, for fear of abandonment. I always feared something might happen when I was away.

My mother remained in the asylum for a month. She returned to our new home and life got back to what I knew as "normal." Again, nothing was ever discussed about her time away; it was treated as if it did not happen. However, from this time forward, my mother would be on medication for the rest of her life. Within months of my mother's homecoming, my father decided the family needed to move to Alabama. This is where his family lived. Therefore, off we went. We moved to Gadsden and rented a house down the street from my father's sister. Mostly what I recall of this time is my mother becoming obsessed with playing bingo and my father drinking each night away. Then, on the weekends, we would visit different aunts. The adults drank and played cards, while my sister and I played with our cousins.

Insecurities controlled my emotions. I remember being ten years old and afraid to be without my parents. One particular time, my parents went out to eat and they dropped my sister and me off at a cousin's house. I was terrified that my parents would not return to pick me up. This type of anxiety consumed me. In the midst of all this darkness, we would visit the house of my father's younger sister, Aunt Faye. Her house was a symbol of hope amongst the rest of his family. She was precious. She was dark-headed and had warm brown eyes. When she smiled, it lit up a room. I have wonderful memories of Aunt Faye. She was the epitome of a southern belle. Always glad when you came to visit, Aunt Faye never spoke a harsh word about anyone, even though most of her family members were alcoholics. Her dinners were feasts. There would be fried chicken or fish, mashed potatoes and gravy, fried okra and corn on the cob, and homemade biscuits. Uncle Jonnie would get out the ice cream maker and make us the yummiest treats. I can still taste it! Being with them was a real safe haven. The love of the Lord permeated their home. I always felt safe with her. She made everyone feel loved.

I had another cousin who was a Christian. Her name was Joann. I did not know her very well, but she was my Aunt Opal's daughter. I recall that her house was immaculate. She had wood floors throughout her house. She had a shine on her wood floors that was unbelievable. I was able to see my reflection in them! Joann was married and had two or three boys. She collected Golden Flake potato chips bags and purchased items with these bags from the company. Joann worked feverishly at saving these bags. She had thousands of these bags! I do not recall how many were needed to purchase certain items, but she was able to get a bicycle for each of her children. After she purchased those bikes, she even had enough left over to purchase one more: one for me. I was thrilled! I received a brand new bike! That bike was the coolest. It was one of the best presents. It was purple and white with a banana seat. (Those banana seats were the coolest thing back in the early 1970s.) The handlebars were ape-hanger, like on the "choppers" of the day. I spent many hours riding that bike. My bike was my most treasured possession.

Not long after I received that bike we left Alabama, (I assume my father was probably running from his bills or from himself) and moved back to Pittsburg, Kansas. We moved into a small apartment where we shared a restroom with the other occupants. My mother decided to get back in church. Unfortunately, she returned to the same legalistic church, probably because it was familiar to her. Life went on, and we attended regularly. My father attended occasionally.

The Lord was trying to intervene in my family. I can vividly recall one day in particular. I remember hearing a sermon about being a sinner and needing a Savior. I recognized this message was for me. Before I knew it, I walked down the aisle and asked the Lord to come into my life. I cried out to Him to forgive me with tears streaming down my cheeks. I had an amazing experience with Jesus; I truly felt His presence. I felt clean for the first time in my life.

It was not long after my decision to follow Christ that the enemy attacked me right at my heart. One Sunday we got ready for church as usual, except I noticed my mother and father were not speaking to one another. Of course my father stayed home and pouted. After church we came home thinking he might have lunch ready. To our surprise, my father was not in the apartment. At first we did not know where he was. I decided to go for a bike ride on my new bike. I thought I would ride down the road to get away. I loved to bike-ride for hours, getting lost in my thoughts. I went to the place where I kept my bike, but to my surprise it was not there anymore. I ran into the house to tell my mother that my bike was missing. Somehow, I knew immediately that my father had taken the bike. Then it dawned on me to look for my rented school cornet. It too was gone, just vanished. We were all convinced that he had taken them to the pawn shop. I wondered, "Where was the money going to take him?" Who knows where? What did it matter? No matter how he justified it, my heart was shattered.

My bike was gone. At eleven, a bike is about the most important possession a child can own. A bike is a means of transportation—a vehicle for endless hours of exploration. Another world awaits a child on a bike, but now that world, for me, was gone.

I cried for hours, the type of crying that leaves one gasping for air until crying is no longer possible. I was too young and wounded to understand how much my father's addiction controlled him, so much so that he would steal from his own daughter. Saddest of all, in God's design a father is to be the one who protects and provides, the most trustworthy person in a child's life. It would be years before I could see that it was Satan, and not my dad, who was the true enemy. Satan came to steal. He was the real thief behind every stolen moment in my life.

The thief comes only in
order to steal and kill and destroy. I came
that they may have and enjoy life, and

have it in abundance (to the full, till it overflows).

John 10:10 (AMP)

Then my struggle with my father went even further. What I was learning at church did not connect with the reality of my home life; we were learning the Ten Commandments, but I found that I could not honor my father anymore. How could a father do the things he did? Keeping the Ten Commandments seemed to be an impossibility to me. How is a child supposed to honor her father if he is a thief and an alcoholic?

I was in a quandary that only God could walk me through. All I knew at the time was that my father had hurt me too many times! I wanted to hate, not honor. I was confused and devastated. I felt the hot dagger of hatred in my heart instead of love, respect, and honor. All I could honestly feel for my father was contempt.

How I wished my mother could have comforted me, but that never happened. My mother was too consumed by her own sadness, and comforting me was beyond her capabilities. I just wanted her to wrap her loving mother's arms around me and say, "Everything is going to be all right. We still have God." However, what I wanted was beyond my reach, because all the stresses of life had taken their toil on my mother. She was merely surviving in such a state of hopelessness that she had nothing left to give. Unfortunately, she did not even have good church support that could have strengthened and healed her or given her encouragement. She must have felt completely alone. That is the worst place a woman can be.

Somehow I innately knew this because I too felt alone, all by myself in a great big world. My mother could not see past her own hurt to see mine. My father had stolen from me, and as time went on I discovered that he struggled with pedophilia. This information made me feel eerie and shameful. I had to carry these feelings around with me; I had no Christian mentor to talk to.

Even though our church was aware of the problems with my abusive father, they ostracized my mother after she filed for a divorce. Having no support from the church, it did not take much for my mother to resort back to a life of sin. She had been in and out of church most of her life, and at this time she seemed to think, "Why bother?" and so she simply gave up. Sad to say, the people in the bars were more supportive of her circumstances than the people in the church! Church folk just did not realize the incredible power they had to love and heal our family; a little love might have worked miracles in this type of situation. Our life could have been so different. It is easy to forget that Christ came to heal the brokenhearted. My mother, my sister, and I were all victims of broken hearts!

My mother felt isolated by her church, and Satan once again succeeded in deceiving her. It is sad when many born again believers buy into his goods of loneliness, hopelessness, and despair. This is one of his favorite schemes; he knows people cannot perpetuate the gospel while living in this defeated state of mind. My mother was victimized by Satan's lies, and she was caught hook, line, and sinker. However, this was not God's plan for her. Beloved, God is the God of hope. God says:

> Such hope never disappoints or deludes
> or shames us, for God's love has been poured
> out in our hearts through the Holy Spirit Who
> has been given to us.
> While we were yet in weakness
> [powerless to help ourselves],
> at the fitting time Christ died for
> (in behalf of) the ungodly

Romans 5:5 (AMP)

After the divorce, my mother started a dramatic and immediate transformation. She became self-absorbed and individualistic, and lost all her motherly instincts (what little she had). Rarely was a meal prepared, and she never took the time to teach us how to do laundry or cook. She would get frustrated, though, when she came home and found these duties not completed. We eventually learned, by trial and error, how to do a few basic household tasks. When it came right down to it, my sister and I were raising ourselves.

To provide for us, my mother worked as a day cook in a facility for the mentally handicapped and at night in a bar. What little free time she had, she certainly did not want to spend it with us. I assume it was probably easier to avoid the problems at home by being gone, and with this avoidance, she was able to ignore the existence of her painful life.

It was a desperate situation — all of us needing love — and we thought it could not be found within our home. I would have given anything to have a family like those on *Leave It to Beaver, The Waltons,* or *Andy Griffith.* The parents in those TV families communicated with their children; they hugged and encouraged them. I longed for someone to hold me and tell me things would work out. I so longed for stability in my life: a father who had a consistent job and a mother who was happy. This desire was only a distant dream in the midst of my nightmare.

Meantime I, too, was changing. I was becoming more defiant, and I had no one to talk to about my pain. This produced a state of confusion in my mind, just as I was becoming a teenager. I was a distressed young girl, a life at risk, ready for trouble.

CHAPTER TWO

Building the Walls of the Prison: The Teen Years

—❦—

Sing to God, sing praise to his name,
extol him who rides on the clouds —
his name is the LORD —
and rejoice before him.
A father to the fatherless, a defender of widows,
is God in his holy dwelling.
God sets the lonely in families,
he leads forth the prisoners with singing;
but the rebellious live in a sun-scorched land.

Psalm 68:4-6 (NIV)

If you are an ordinary teen, life is difficult enough to process, but I had a wounded spirit that added another dimension of complexity. I was coming of age, but was totally bewildered about life. I was a child of divorce. Church was out of the question, in my opinion, and I was struggling with failure in school. Hurt and pain consumed my heart. Life was so unpredictable, and I reacted in ways that even I did not understand. Envy became a way of life for me as I watched plenty of my fellow teens growing up in "normal" environments.

I felt cheated. Why wasn't I born into a family that loved one another? I was angry with God and even angrier with myself. I was an emotional mess. Yet my acting skills had been refined, for no one knew what was going on inside me. My wounds were old and buried deep inside, yet burned as though they were fresh. At times, I would explode and start yelling at everyone in sight, not understanding the root of my infirmity. My reactions were a precise mirror of how my mother would react to any given situation. I fell prey to the enemy's scheme, and I carried that generational curse with a passion.

During this period, life consisted of going to school and babysitting my younger sister. I was not able to play sports or be involved in activities like other teens. No, it became my responsibility to take care of my little sister. My mother was always working or bar hopping. My father had not changed his behavior; it was business as usual. He was in and out of our lives. "Family" consisted pretty much of just my sister and me, and instead of this pulling us closer together, I saw her as a hindrance, the one who limited my right to freedom.

A few friends at school were aware of my precarious home situation and came to hang out with me. They loved the fact that I was able to smoke at home with my parents' permission. They considered my mother "cool." It did not take long for word to spread that my home was unsupervised. Soon several "throw away" teens were gathered at my house. The house was a place where drugs, music, and sex ruled. Everyone was searching for a feeling of belonging. My home became the "Heartbreak Hotel." It was a place of refuge where too many found companionship and acceptance of the wrong kind. Now that I am older, I look back on this time and think, "Where were these other kids' parents?" What happened to parenting in our society in the 1970s? (One of my friends literally lived with us. She had a mother and a father who were still married, yet she spent at least five to six nights a week at our house. Even though we never discussed it, I know she felt abandoned as well. Her parents each worked a couple of jobs and were never home.)

With a party atmosphere at my home three or four nights a week, academic studies were the least of my priorities. School became a place to make contacts with friends and discuss what we were going to do at night. Any sort of relationship with God was far removed from my lifestyle. Walking with the Lord was something I was convinced could not happen and still allow me to enjoy life. I was so wrapped up in my wild existence that I thought this lifestyle was the ticket for the much sought-after teenage independence.

Just as I was becoming more self-consumed, so was my mother. She let a friend of hers live with us for a few months. This infuriated me. It seemed like they were two teenage girls, and suddenly I had become the unwanted younger sister. My mother's entire attention went to her friend and her entertainment. Her friend despised me, with due reason. First, I had been one that would speak my mind to anyone, including her. Second, I was so full of anger towards my mother that my resentment came out in various forms of disrespect. I was frustrated with my family and felt betrayed by all of them. Silently, I was crying for help, but all I received was disapproval thrown back at me. I constantly heard how bad I was, and that no one was going to like me. My mother and her friend frequently reminded me, "You will never amount to anything." These words penetrated my being. Their motivation scheme did not inspire me, but instead backfired and drove me into believing that failure was my destiny. Yet saddest of all, I responded to my little sister in the same way I had been treated. This destructive behavior was being passed on from person to person. It took many years to break the power of this bondage. It was a stronghold, and it haunted me for years. Thank God, Jesus breaks strongholds!

Mother dated a few men here and there. She had the decency to keep her sex life away from the house. Many times she would return home early in the morning. However, a few of her man friends did come around. There was one in particular whom I really did not care for although, oddly enough, he liked me. He made it obvious that he did not care for my younger sister, Tonda, however. His actions toward her angered me. In hindsight, I always wondered, "Did my mother notice how he and her other 'boyfriends' treated us?" On the other hand, maybe she was so wrapped up in her own loneliness that she lived in oblivion. Whatever the reason, I resented her for this too. As resentment increased, I fell into deeper rebellion.

What I really hungered for most was a true relationship with my mother. I would have given anything for her to hug me, and tell me she loved me, and encourage me. I wanted her to believe in me and not think of me as her "problem." Sadly, this was not to be. If she "mothered" us at all, it was usually over the phone. She would try to tell us what to do as she was coming and going. She even tried to handle some of our crazy arguments via the phone! My sister, Karen, whom we lived with during my mother's breakdown, was now divorced, and she came over quite often. She was constantly on my case about how I treated mother and what I needed to do. She often told me how immature I was. As a typical fifteen-year-old, I did not care what she thought! If Karen and I argued, my mother typically sided with her, so it seemed to me that I was the odd one out. I am sure I frustrated my mother, because I called her on her actions many times. Needless to say, unity was not in our family!

One day my mother and I got into a very heated argument, and out of her frustration she looked at me and cried out, "I wish that you never would have been born! If you weren't here, I could be finished raising children and I would be free." Her words went through my heart like a hot knife. I had always felt rejected, and now she had verbalized it.

I thought to myself. "I didn't ask to be born. It is not my fault." There were many times in my life I questioned God as to why I was even born. This hurt propelled me into further rebellion against my mother, but again, deep inside, I was screaming for her love and acceptance. Why didn't my own mother love me?

It was impossible for me to see that my mother had literally quit her job as a mother, and she had abandoned us emotionally. If we were not home alone, then we were left with our father. My mother was fully aware of his past behavior, and I am not sure why she subjected my sister and me to this dangerous situation. It was only a matter of time before we found out firsthand his struggles with pedophilia.

This nightmare began one evening when my little niece, my younger sister, a friend and I were to stay the night at my father's duplex. It was Friday night, so I decided to go out with friends first. We went riding around, had a few drinks, and popped some pills. In short order, I was what you would call "wasted." When I returned to my father's place, I was beginning to come down from the high caused by these potent drugs. Needless to say, I wasn't quite "all there." It was between 11:30 p.m. and 12:00 a.m. All the lights were out. I assumed everyone was asleep. I put blanket pallets on the floor for my friend and me to sleep on. However, I could not sleep; I was still a little wired from the drugs. I talked a little to my friend about the evening. Then all of a sudden, I heard the sound of my niece's weeping coming from my father's bedroom. I strained and heard her plead, "Grandpa, don't." An eerie feeling came over me, and I knew exactly what was taking place behind those doors. My stomach twisted in knots. I knew I needed to do something, but I did not know what. I hesitated and asked God to intervene. At once, we got up and ran to the nearest convenience store to use the pay phone. I called my mother for help. We waited at the convenience store for about twenty-five minutes. My mother loaded us up and we went to salvage the little ones. By the time we returned to my father's duplex, he had vanished, on the run again. This was the story of his life.

Anger rose up in my spirit. I knew he was drunk, but it was no excuse. I felt nothing but disdain for him. I had forgiven him for many grievances, but this was pure evil. How could he commit such an atrocity? What was wrong with him? Not only did I have malevolent thoughts for him, I was not too pleased with my mother either. I thought, *How could she put us in this precarious situation in the first place?*

The weight of guilt and shame burdened me for many years, as somehow I also felt responsible for his actions that night. I buried it deep in my soul. I often wondered, "What if I had stayed at the duplex?" The knowledge of my father's pedophilia was very painful to me, so painful, in fact, that I did not mention it to anyone in or outside of family. Whom can you confide in when your father is a pedophile? I just wanted all this to go away.

It was as though I carried my family's shame with me everywhere I went. It was about this time I realized that my family was dreadfully messed up. My sister and I desperately needed someone to save us from the destructive path of our parents. We needed a rescuer, but none was to be found. We were left to fend for ourselves.

One day I went over to a friend's house. Visiting her family were her relatives from Illinois. We were sitting around, talking, when suddenly a stranger entered the room. We were taken with each other instantly. He had dark hair and olive-toned skin, and he looked Italian. He was mysterious to me. He was a little older than I was, and he seemed to know a great deal about many subjects I was interested in. I was fascinated that he was from a "big city." He had a deep, rich voice with a great Chicagoan accent. I felt as though I had found a very special friend.

At first, he treated me like a princess. He paid attention to me, wrote me love letters, even poetry. He nicknamed me "precious." He was protective of me, something I had never experienced before. My high school days became filled with expectations of what would be waiting for me in the mail when I came home. At least two times a month I would find a package waiting for me at the door. It was like Christmas twice a month! Each package would be filled with amusing things: a letter, tapes, record albums, and knickknacks. Better yet, joy came with each package.

On the home front, tensions were on the rise. It seemed as if I could not do anything right. My mother was always nagging me about what I "was not." I knew I was a disappointment to her. Then one day I could not take anymore. It was September of 1978; she began to yell at me and put me down. I yelled back at her with spiteful words. My sister Karen decided to get in the thick of it. In the heat of the argument, I was told to get my things and leave! I was fifteen and homeless! At once, I called my friend in Chicago. Through my tears, I gave details about the fight that had just taken place. His mother had compassion on me and suggested I come and live with her. I knew I needed a change. Anyway, what other option did I have? Off I went to Chicago. At first, I assumed this was an answer to one of my prayers. My boyfriend's mother wanted a daughter, and I needed a mother. It was a perfect match! Violet, my boyfriend's mother, was a wonderful person. She was good to me. In the end, I do not know if I was more infatuated with my friend or his mother! It was hard to tell. I was so attention-starved for someone out there to love me, just anyone, and Violet did a good job!

A couple of days after that phone call, I found myself on a plane, headed for the Big City! Flying was a stimulating experience for me. Travel and meeting people was fun! It was exhilarating to fly into O'Hare airport, with all the different people going to fascinating places. The sights mesmerized me; much like my mother had been when she met my father. Like her, I assumed I was escaping the pain. The pain was at home, and I had left it behind (or so I thought).

When I arrived in Chicago, they greeted me with great excitement. I could not believe someone actually wanted me around. I thought to myself, "I am finally going to have a real family." Little did I know this family had their own dysfunctional behaviors. Dysfunction comes in many different packages. This family appeared to have it together, and granted they were a lot more functional than mine was, but they also had their share of problems. I was soon to discover that they also were wounded and needed the Lord to heal them. Christ is the only Savior, and no one escapes his or her need for Him.

In the meantime, however, I found my life radically changed overnight. All of a sudden, I went from a small town high school in Kansas to a mega school in the suburbs of Chicago. Life was exciting. I took my small-town demeanor to the big city, and people in Chicago were astounded by my friendliness, finding me instantly approachable. This carried over into the neighborhood in which I was staying. Like many city dwellers, this family had not taken the time to meet most of their neighbors; they were caught up in city life. Before they knew it, I had met most of their neighbors, and I knew many of them by name. This took everyone by surprise and became the joke of the house!

At first I was so happy to be with them. They immediately treated me as if I were their very own. They were kind to me, and they fixed up the extra room for me. I felt wanted. However, I was a self-absorbed teenager, and many times I became aggravated with Violet when she made me do my homework and laundry. This was unusual to me; my mother never verified if I had done my homework. I was just told to do it, but Vi was on top of her house. I could not get away with much!

Of course, this was exactly what I needed: a mother to watch over me, train me, and correct me with love. When she made me do my homework and kept me accountable, I felt much more secure, because subconsciously I knew she cared. She would work all day and them come home and fix a wonderful dinner. As many families do, we sat down at the table to eat dinner. This tradition had been missing from my house for many years. After my parents' divorce, anything that resembled normalcy at dinnertime had ceased.

There was one wonderful day I will never forget. It was a Saturday, and the day began with Violet and me doing chores. After we finished, Violet looked at me and exclaimed, "Let's go shopping!" We got in the car and off we went to the department store. When we walked in the doors, she instantly went to the junior department. She looked at me and said, "Pick a few things out; I am going to buy you some new clothes!" She went to the racks and thumbed through them, picking items out and telling me, "Here, try this on, this will look nice on you," and, "Pam, you are such a pretty girl." These words were like honey to my soul. Rarely did anyone speak positively to me. I ended up getting two complete outfits that day. When I say "complete" I mean the shirts, pants to match and even new shoes! (I do not recall ever having a day like this with my own mother. If I needed a shirt or jeans, she gave me the money and I went to Wal-Mart to get them.) When Violet and I finished shopping, we went out to lunch. We sat down and talked. She was truly interested in me. She wanted to know about school, my friends, and how things were going between her son and me. I remember that lunch being especially delicious, maybe because of the company instead of the food! We giggled the day away. Mother-daughter relationships were foreign to me, and even now,

I still cherish that day. I was longing for a mother, and she played the role brilliantly.

Violet and Bill tried to provide a good home for their son. They both worked hard and provided financially. Inside that home, however, Bill drank nightly. Their son was popping pills every weekend, and even persuaded me to consume potent drugs with him. The irony in all of this was that he was protective of me in so many ways, but on the other hand, he was giving me narcotics. None of this made sense. Drugs and alcohol became synonymous with the word "weekend." It is amazing I have a brain cell left! Even as I did this, it bothered me that my boyfriend was "escaping" reality, too. Why was he running? What was he trying to escape?

Even though I was deep in this sin and felt guilty about my actions, I still did not stop. I continued in my sin. God would speak to me occasionally about coming back to Him. I ignored the call and went on with my life. I thought to myself, "Someday, when I am older, I will come back." Amazingly, God never left me. As I look back, I realize that His hand was on me. Many dreadful outcomes could have happened to me but they did not, and I believe it is because there was a covering on me. Paul quotes in Hebrews 13:5, "Never will I leave you; never will I forsake you" (NIV).

God said it, and I have lived it! I do know this is true in my life!

The dark side of this family was about to be revealed. After about five months, issues began to get progressively worse. Bill, the father, was a functioning alcoholic. This was nothing like my father's binge drinking. No, Bill was able to keep a good paying job, and he stayed with his wife. Many times he had too much to drink and got a little demanding with Violet. She knew how to handle him most of the time. His moods were capricious after he had been drinking; so you could never guess them. He might be a big teddy bear, loving and kind, or he could turn into an ugly old grizzly bear, ready to attack and rip you apart!

One evening Bill "the grizzly" came home after dinner and seemed especially grumpy. I knew to stay clear and went to my room. I felt nervous, so I decided to turn the light outs and lie in bed. I could hear him fuss at Violet in the kitchen. He was being a hateful tyrant. She tried to calm him down, but this time she lost the battle. He became more belligerent the more she pleaded with him to stop. I overheard her say, "Stop Bill, Pam is going to hear you!" That statement propelled him into uncontrollable anger. He began to use all kinds of profanity and shouted at her, "I don't give a d— — who hears me, this is my house." Then it got personal. He called me a f— — — b— — and then he called my mother a f— —- whore. I heard every word, and his words knifed deeply into my heart. I got up and hid in the closet of my room. I shut the door, curled into a fetal position, and began to weep. I cried profusely for hours. Their arguing seemed to go on forever. The pain of his accusation was immense. Finally, he went to bed. When it was over, I numbly got up and crawled into my bed. However, something had changed forever inside me, and another layer of wounds was added to my heart. I knew I would be moving on again soon.

When he was sober, Bill apologized to me and begged me not to leave. I was not sure where his anger might take him next, and I did not want to be in harm's way. I decided against staying and returned home. I had made many bad choices in the past, but this one seemed right. Something told me not to stay. I came to this conclusion during my time in the closet.

After six months in Chicago, here I was, homeward bound. Overall, the time there was certainly not wasted. Violet taught me how to clean house. She also taught me a few things about cooking. Most importantly, she taught me how to have a mother-daughter relationship. She helped me become a tad more functional than I had been before. To this day, I am very grateful for what she tried to do in my life.

When I returned to living with my mother, situations were a little better than before. I began to do my homework on a regular basis. My grades improved slightly, though not as much as they should have. I still could not read and write very well. I remained involved in drug activity. Nevertheless, brighter moments were on the way. Miraculously, I got a job in a nice department store. This helped my developing social skills. I was around people who were a lot more functional than I had ever been. The people had normal relationships where everyone was not arguing all the time. This job made it possible for me to purchase a car. My life was getting better; the windows of the world were opening up for me. I started to see that I did not have to live as my family had done. The determination to be different from my family became a growing motivation and played a huge role in my life.

Even though I was maturing and was hardly ever around the house, pleasing my mother remained an impossible task. She always accused me of silly trifles. She was very paranoid that I was going to take advantage of her, which I never did. She worried constantly about things I might do that never came to fruition. This made it very difficult for us to live together. Some of my other siblings had left her with diffi-cult situations financially, but I never had. Still, she began to complain more and more about me, and my attitude was not the least bit respectful toward her. It was ugly! Finally, my sister Sherry came to my rescue. I moved in with her in my junior year of high school.

My sister Sherry was going through a horrible time, for her husband had just died of cancer and she had two small children to raise. We decided to move in together. Unfortunately, though I could have been such a great help, I was a very self-centered teen at this time and I doubt that I helped her much at all. She was in despair, but she was still reaching out to help me. I am so grateful now for the help she offered to me then.

My dear sister was wounded from her past, too, and now she had to deal with widowhood on top of it. She, like me, was looking for ways to escape. She began to join my life of sin. We both began looking for love in a bar, the worst place possible! We just lived for the moment, and life was about entertainment only. My weekends were spent inoculating pain.

To complicate things, my friend from Chicago moved down to my small town. He attended the local college. We dated for a while, but he quickly became too controlling and demanding. His behavior became very similar to his father's. I was not that same little girl he had once dated. I had been on my own for too long to let anyone control me. I was not passive about this issue, and we began to fight often. Then I started to see signs of alcoholism in him. One night when we were over at some friends' house, we were drinking gin and tonic. The demeanor of my friend changed; he transformed before my eyes into a different person altogether. He began to say spiteful things. I was humiliated by his behavior, became angry, and wanted to leave. This was the end for us. From that moment, I began to distance myself from him.

Then one night he came looking for me after he had too much to drink. He came to my house and we began to argue. Suddenly, he grabbed me violently and threatened to hit me! Miraculously, I got away, slipped out of my house, and ran for safety to another apartment. This person gave me shelter until we were sure he had gone away. If he had caught me, I have no idea what would have transpired. I think he would have hurt me badly and then regretted it when he sobered up, just as his father had done two years before.

As I look back on this event, I am saddened because he had been so good to me in earlier times. The effects of alcohol were too prevalent to ignore. At one time, he even told me he loved me and wanted to be with me forever. I truly believed him, and even believed that I loved him too. Nevertheless, had we stayed together, we would have destroyed each other. Our relationship was far from healthy.

At present, I have been able to forgive and even pray that the Lord blesses him. The Lord is the only One who can heal his wounded heart. Once again, I saw the evidence of God's protective hand in my life. Honestly, the situation of that one horrible night could have been fatal.

This relationship haunted me for many years. This man had an emotional hold on me, yet I knew I had to leave him behind. A few months later, I began to date a friend's older brother from school. It was another unhealthy relationship that I came to regret deeply. In many ways it was very similar to the previous one. This person had been abandoned by his father and was looking for comfort, just as I was. Our relationship was nothing but a tumultuous, constant battle. To be honest, not all of our arguments were his fault; I know for a fact I caused many of them. As crazy as it may sound, at one time we too thought of marriage! Now that is desperation! This relationship lasted about eight months and then we broke up. He immediately began to date another girl that I attended high school with. She was jealous of me, which I never understood. She stalked me, which made me very nervous until I finally approached her one day and said, "Look, I am not a threat to you; he and I are over." She had no idea how thankful I was to be out of that relationship! I could recognize the warning signs; my life would have been an even bigger mess than it already was! I just wanted to move on. As I look back on these two individuals and the mess I was in, I see such hopelessness. My choices in men had been just like my mother's. These relationships would have brought endless amounts of sorrow in my life, just as my mother's relationships had. Again, I could have gone down a most dangerous path, but the arm of the Lord was guiding me when I did not even acknowledge it.

Even though I was glad to be out of this relationship, it brought fresh disappointments into my life. For a period, I was convinced healthy relationships were impossible. I really don't think I knew the low mental and moral condition I was in. I would have given anything for a mentor in my life at that time, a positive influence, someone to teach me about the Lord and what He wanted to accomplish in me. I wished I could have known this verse in Jeremiah:

For I know the thoughts and plans that
I have for you, says the Lord, thoughts and plans for
welfare and peace and not for evil, to give you hope in
your final outcome.

Jeremiah 29:11 (AMP)

At this time in my life, this verse was probably beyond my realm of comprehension. I felt so worthless; I couldn't have comprehended why God would have good plans for me. I was a wretched sinner. I was a failure in life. All my relationships were temporary. When I did think of the Lord, I immediately felt guilt and condemnation. My only solace in life was to party. I was not about to give up my partying for anyone. I was just so blind.

By now, I had been out of school a year and was struggling with my self-esteem. I hung out at the bar on weekends, drinking and wondering if I would ever find "Mr. Right." I was one of those girls who always wanted a boyfriend, as if I was not complete unless I had a man. But rarely did I have one. It was strange. I guess I was longing for love and was so convinced he would be 6-feet tall, have dark hair and deep brown eyes, and drive a nice car to boot!

I still lived with my sister, Sherry, but she had begun dating someone seriously. I had some friends that wanted me to move in with them. Eventually, I moved in with these girls, but I lived with them for only six months. I never knew where my next home would be. I had become a young adult, but my life was so transient that I kept belongings at my mother's and my sister's houses. Nothing was permanent in my life; I was adrift.

The winds of change were blowing strongly; tossing me around like tumbleweed. I was a lost soul, wandering. A metamorphosis was taking place in me physically, but emotionally I was stagnating.

CHAPTER THREE

Cinderella: A Ray of Hope!

All night long on my bed
I looked for the one my heart loves;
I looked for him but did not find him.
I will get up now and go about the city,
through its streets and squares;
I will search for the one my heart loves.
So I looked for him but did not find him.
The watchmen found me
as they made their rounds in the city.
"Have you seen the one my heart loves?"
Scarcely had I passed them
when I found the one my heart loves.

Song of Solomon 3:1-4 (NIV)

Now that I had graduated from high school, I wondered what I was going to do with my life. I was clueless. All I knew was that I wanted my future to be very different from my past, but I did not know how to achieve that difference. I did not believe I was bright enough for college. It seemed the only thing I did well was party, and so partying is what I did. I lived for Wednesday and weekend nights.

There was one Wednesday night when I happened to be in my usual hangout, a college one at that. My friends and I went there in pursuit of finding good dates. Within an hour, the place was teeming with people. My friends and I were mingling in the crowd with a drink in one hand and a smoke in the other. In my peripheral vision, I could see a cute, dark-haired, brown-eyed guy approaching my friend. He called her by name. I listened from a distance. He asked her, "Who is the girl in the red shirt?" Somehow, I knew he was inquiring about me. Not only did I have a red shirt on, but also our eyes had met earlier. So of course I found his inquiry intriguing. My curiosity rose, and my heart started to palpitate. I wondered, "What would he want with *me?*" My girlfriend called me over and introduced me to Randy. My attraction to him was immediate. He had a charm about him that almost seemed like he was a young boy with a whimsical sense of humor. That is probably what attracted me most to him. We continued to talk way into the evening, and he asked to take me home. As I entered my sister's house, I was floating on air. I went into Sherry's bedroom and proceeded to tell her about my evening. For the first time ever, I was truly captivated by a guy. Later, I learned that the same had happened to him. Randy went home that evening to his parents' house and told his mother, "I have met the girl I want to marry."

After that night, Randy and I began to date. I was wild about him. He was just exciting to be around. I never knew what to expect! He lived life on the edge, like a wild mustang running freely on the open plain. He became a challenge to me; he was so hard to second guess. He fascinated me, and I loved his thrill-seeking personality.

Even though Randy and I came from completely different backgrounds, we had a few commonalties. He too just wanted to have a good time. His life consisted of going to college, working on the weekend, and partying. It seemed as though he also suffered emotional pain from the past, and he wanted to avoid further pain at any cost. In many ways, we were just two lost souls looking for attention.

Two weeks prior to our meeting, tragedy had hit Randy's family. His brother had been in a terrible car accident and was in a coma. Randy mentioned the accident occasionally, and when he did, I could see he was deeply concerned for his brother, Dwight. One night Randy picked me up for a date; he decided that we should go to the hospital to visit Dwight. I had heard so much about him, I was glad Randy thought enough of me to take me for a visit. As soon as we went in Dwight's room, I could see Randy's countenance change. It was heartwarming and gut wrenching all at the same time. His mother greeted us with joy. She asked me to sign Dwight's guestbook. She kept track of everyone who visited so that when Dwight woke up, he would know how loved he was. From my perspective, signing that guestbook was an act of faith.

I stood in the back of the room and kept a respectful distance. As Dwight lay there in a coma, I watched Randy approach him. Randy took his hand and began to talk to him as if Dwight could hear and answer. I could see the tears in Randy's eyes; his heart was broken. His love for his brother was obviously very deep. It was my first peek into Randy's sensitive side, and one of the very few I was ever to see until Christ came into Randy's life much later. When we left the hospital, he was quiet for some time. His pain was intense, and all he wanted to do was cry, but he was afraid to let his emotions flow freely. I decided to keep quiet and just let him assess his thoughts.

The visit to the hospital was a pivotal point in my feelings for Randy. I admired his genuine love for his brother. At that time in my life, I had not really experienced that kind of compassion for a sibling. Everyone in my family was in survival mode, trying to pick up the pieces of their own brokenness. I think in my family, pain was so commonplace and on the surface, that avoidance was a defense mechanism used for survival.

Randy and I continued to date, and eventually I met his whole family (Randy is the second child out of six). His family seemed ideal: everyone was attending or planning to attend college. Even his parents had a college education. His parents were still together. His father ran the family company that had been in business for over seventy years. I saw his father have a drink only on a few occasions, and to top that off, Randy had lived in one house the entire time he grew up! It was unreal to me that anyone could be that stable!

This family was like a living scene out of *Leave It to Beaver.* My word, they communicated with each other around the dinner table! (My meals consisted of frozen dinners in a chair watching *One Day at a Time.*) Certainly, this had to be the answer to my prayers; it was just the kind of family I had longed for. I convinced myself that he was the one for me. I began to see Randy as my ticket out of my pitiful life. It was not long after I met his family that I became determined to marry him.

After a year of dating Randy, my father was hospitalized with cirrhosis of the liver. The stress began building in my life. I looked to Randy for comfort, but he saw the pain in my life and really wanted no part of it. Pain was an emotion he wanted to avoid, and he was just not able to console me. Once again, I was on my own. I simply accepted the fact that my pain was mine and mine alone.

My father got progressively worse. I watched this man's health deteriorate before my eyes. His once olive skin had become yellow and pale. His beautiful gray eyes had become dull and glazed over. All the years of alcohol abuse had finally caught up with him, and death was imminent. Even though I was not living for the Lord, I knew I needed to call a pastor in to pray with him. I wanted to make sure he was right before he saw his Creator.

God, in His grace, made sure my dad was aware of his fate. A few days before my father took his last breath, we were all gathered in his room; the only one missing was my sister Karen. With struggling speech, he looked up at all of us and whispered, "I am sorry for all the things I have done to all of you." What a beautiful moment that God so graciously gave us. His hand was evident that day. God was starting the healing process. Even though we all were clueless at the time, I did find much comfort in knowing that my father had made peace with God. Yet, I still wanted to hold on to my unforgiving attitude, as though it was my right. Little did I know that in order to be healed myself, I would one day have to let that go.

As my father gasped his last breath, I sat there looking out the window, thinking, "This really can't be happening." My heart wanted to be a million miles away from this moment; I did not want to feel the pain or even feel anything, for that matter. This man had brought so much hurt to my family, and now he was pleading for his life. I turned my head and watched the pain and suffering he had endured for so long finally end. He was gone and it was over. He was in eternity.

It is a rare experience to watch a person breathe their last breath. After his death, I felt relief more than sadness. I was glad his torment was over. He had struggled for so long with his addictions and his sin. I could feel the pain of the past trying to surface, but I slammed a lid on it and refused to feel anything. My heart was like a rock.

After my father's death, my relationship with Randy went on as though nothing had happened. Randy and I started to have a few problems. He wanted to change me. He had an image of what his wife was to be and he tried to force me to become that. He started to look at my faults and complain a lot about my shortcomings. I was so insecure at the time; I began to do anything to please him. He began to pressure me to attend college. I had no desire to go to college, yet I went anyway. I enrolled in a few classes, and as I expected, I did not do well at all. I could not see any value for me in a college education. I attended for Randy's approval. Since this was my motivation, I did not make my studies a priority. After receiving my first set of grades, I was convinced that everything I already felt about myself was true. I thought I was worthless. Of course, I had not tried too terribly hard either, but I still felt shame. My reading skills were so poorly developed that I was functionally illiterate, so college seemed an impossible task to me, just like finding someone to love me for who I was.

My failure to succeed in academics disappointed Randy, but we continued to date. His mother encouraged our relationship, even our marriage. She saw how crazy I was for Randy. She became convinced I was the "right one" for her son.

Randy happened to be in his last year of college. He wanted nothing more than to be hired by a big company and climb the corporate ladder. His plans were to move away, go to the big city. I believe that he cared for me, but there was also a sense that he "settled" for me. I am not saying he did not have genuine affection for me. I am sure he did, but he did not possess real love for me. It seemed that he listened to his mother and did what she wanted him to do, and that was to marry me.

Of course, my reasons for marriage were just as wretched. I married him for the wrong reasons as well. Sure, I was crazy about him, but I also saw him as a means of escape. He was my ticket out; I would never have to return to my mother's house. Naturally, no one realized how much pain from the past I had buried, especially me. Nothing was going to work for me until I dealt with my own sin and the past. I was oblivious to just how much of my life was going to be affected by all of this.

With this mixture of hidden agendas between us, off to the wedding chapel we went! Even though my motives were selfish, the wedding itself was exquisite. My wedding was a gift that I will cherish forever. Even the weather cooperated; it was a beautiful day in June. God seemed to smile on me that day, for on my wedding day, instead of the forecasted "rain and clouds," the sun came out and the sky was a brilliant blue. Rainfall in the night had been just enough to make the next morning appear fresh, crisp, and flawless.

Randy was his parents' first child to get married and they spared no expense, including the best in flowers, candles, and beautiful music. About 500 people attended. I felt like a "Cinderella." Me, a meager poor girl, got to go to the "ball," and my what a ball! That evening we had a reception at the country club. The club opened their back doors as the sun began to set, and people gathered on the back balcony. A jazz band played in the background, and everyone began to dance. It was perfect.

After the wedding, we stayed in town for our wedding night and then left the next day for Jamaica. My feelings returned to the day we first met, and riding the wave of those first emotions, I floated the week away. The honeymoon was a trip I could never have dreamt of taking. It was beyond my realm of thinking. God's hand was on my life, but I did not give Him any credit. I just knew my life was turning out differently and more wonderfully than I could ever have imagined.

When we returned, though, reality began to sink in. The reality of marriage was a whole different story. A "marriage relationship," day in and day out, is entirely distinct from romance, a fairy tale wedding, and a honeymoon. Now the hard work was about to begin.

CHAPTER FOUR

Marriage, B.C.

—⊂◉⁄⊅—

You hear, O LORD, the desire of the afflicted;
you encourage them, and you listen to their cry ,
defending the fatherless and the oppressed,
in order that man, who is of the earth, may terrify no more.

Psalm 10:17-18 (NIV)

Thinking back on my first few years of marriage is like watching an old black and white movie. I see two actors playing the "husband" and "wife" and they look familiar to me, but my mind is scrambling because it is as if I just cannot recall their names. These same two actors today have changed so much that they do not even look or appear to be the same people. My early years of marriage seem surreal to me, like an old grainy film with subtitles.

The saying "the honeymoon is over" rang true in our life as soon as we returned from Jamaica. We moved into an apartment two days after we returned, and I immediately went to look for a job. I had only a high school education and barely one at that; moving from school to school during my developmental years hurt my academic ability dramatically. I could hardly read or write! However, I *could* sell! Retail was the only job where I could excel. I started my "career" in the cosmetic department at Dillard's. Randy was also employed with Dillard's, and he was in the management trainee program. Randy and I both were a little intimidated by city life. It was an adjustment, with so many choices of stores and restaurants to choose from. We had never experienced such decisions. We were used to about three different department stores, local family owned restaurants, and no "chains" other than fast food in our small town.

Randy was excited about his career. He wanted to go all the way to the top with Dillard's. His dream was to manage one of their big stores. For the first few months, he worked with a buyer and learned the structure of the business. With his gregarious personality, he began to meet people and make friends right away. He was asked to play on a softball team and he accepted. If softball was the only game being played it would have been fine, but Randy also played the "partier" game. He would go out and have a few drinks with the guys. His short-term memory loss kicked in, and it continuously slipped his mind that he should call home and tell me what was going on. He set his own social agenda, and it was treated as though it was none of my business. My dreams of a great marriage and wonderful life vanished in about a month. Those feelings of rejection and depression from my childhood returned. Inevitably, we had many arguments for dinner.

In the midst of this mayhem, he came home one day and announced that he had been transferred to Wichita, Kansas. The news came on Thursday that he had to report for work in Wichita on Monday! We had to pack immediately. The moving truck arrived the next afternoon, ready to be loaded. For me, this was a move made under duress. I had just begun to get adjusted to Ft. Worth, and then suddenly we were moving.

This move was doubly insane as it was only three weeks before Christmas and we needed a place to live. We were desperate! With no place to live, we put our furniture in storage, and for a week, the Best Western Hotel became our little residence. It was too cold and snowy to go out. I remember being bored to death; all I did was watch TV for a week. I guess in the end, this was probably a good thing, because I was so emotionally exhausted I really needed the rest. I did not look for a job yet; I wanted to know where we would live and become settled before starting over.

We had only one car, so Randy had an apartment hunter locate an apartment for us. To my surprise, the apartment was older and not nearly as well kept as the one in Texas. I often wondered what kind of commission the apartment hunter must have received. She told us that there were not many to pick from and that was the best she could do. Of course, we eventually learned otherwise. Anyway, we were homeless and beggars, and "beggars can't be choosers."

Once we moved in, I busied myself putting everything away. Christmas was only two weeks away, and I wanted our first Christmas to be special. I had the whole apartment done within twenty-four hours, even pictures on the wall. The next day I went out and bought a few ornaments and a real tree. It was my first time ever to have a real Christmas tree. My mother and little sister were allergic to pine, and so we never had a real tree.

I got everything done and decided I would wait until January to look for a job. Then right before Christmas, I came down with a sore throat and terrible cold. I simply did not feel well at all. I tried to ignore my symptoms and enjoy the holidays. In fact, we went back to visit our families for Christmas, and even though my activities were limited, it was nice to see everyone. After we returned home, and while still feeling bad from my terrible cold, I came down with a 48-hour bug. I could not keep any food or liquid down. I was bedridden for days. I just could not shake this illness. Here I was alone in Wichita, knowing no one, unable to work or even go out to meet people. I was very moody and depressed.

I was unable to be any support for Randy, and his patience began to wear thin with me. He had no idea how to deal with these kinds of emotions, so he chose to avoid me.

It seemed he came home only when he had to; he was really married to his work. He enjoyed his life at work. He quickly developed many friendships, including one with the manager of the store. His dreams were coming true, and he was on his way. Soon, he was the manager of the men's department.

The responsibilities at home were an unwanted weight. He became very cold and distant to me. We never discussed our situation; it was just easier to ignore.

Finally, after lying around for a month, I started feeling better physically. I knew I needed to get a job or an education. Returning to retail was a dead-end to me, and I did not want to work weekends or nights anymore. Determined to "become something," I decided I wanted to work in an office. I was convinced school was the answer. Anyway, I was not too sure if this marriage was going to work and I knew I had to have a backup plan. I sure could not go back home; there was no home to go to. So once again, it was up to me.

Attending a business college became my love. It assisted me with improving my reading and writing skills. For the first time in my life, I truly enjoyed learning. This business school started to build up a pseudo self esteem in me. What surprised me was that I could actually accomplish something if I applied myself! Not only was I learning, but also I was meeting people. At this school, I became friends with a girl named Lori. We hit it off instantly; she was a lot of fun. We spent a lot of time together. Her marriage was as much of a dead-end as mine. She too had married to escape home, just as I did. Our friendship grew as time passed. We both tried very hard to avoid the pain in our lives by focusing on just having a good time, and that is exactly what we did.

Neither one of us had a job, so after classes, our afternoons were free. Many times, we ventured out to a little Irish pub, drank beer, and shot pool. If we were not at the pub, we went back to my apartment and played cards. It was just Lori and me most of the time. Once in awhile we included our husbands, but rarely. We were self-absorbed and enjoyed "crying in our beer."

Anyway, Randy was busy working and trying to climb the corporate success ladder. He started running around with the manager of the store. He believed this person had the power to expedite his climb. The manager worked very hard but had a terrible cocaine habit; we would not find this out until later, and partying every night was his life. He invited Randy to go to the bars with him at least three times a week. Without hesitation, Randy tagged right along. Of course, Randy rationalized his behavior with the excuse, "If I don't go with him it will affect my job." Only the Lord knows if he was telling the truth. As you can see, my marriage was not about Randy and me. Our ships were docked into different ports most of the time.

I was suspicious of Randy and his manager's antics, but I did not want to face the truth, for I knew his actions could rip my heart apart. "Ignorance is bliss," or so they say. I chose the "bliss." It was easier and more convenient to overlook these shenanigans. I had gotten to the place in my life that it was not worth the arguing. I just wanted to finish school and do my own thing. I could not handle my life as it was, and I was not about to add any more stress to the situation.

Wichita was only three hours from my hometown, so occasionally I would go home to see my friends and sisters. Even though I did not have a home to run to, I was homesick. I had an aching desire to be home, a home that provided a secure and loving environment. I was yearning for someone to love me, hold me tight, and proclaim that everything was going to be all right. I wanted a savior. I was such a vacuum, empty and depleted of any affection. I did not receive it from Randy, so I went to look elsewhere.

In April of 1985, I reached out to my old boyfriend's mother in Chicago. She invited me to come up for the weekend. Desperate for love, I went. I knew her son would be there. I was aware he was part of the package. I was desperate. I did reach out to him. It too was a disappointment. He treated me as if I was that fifteen-year-old girl he had once known. That did not go over too well with me. I was twenty-one at the time and wanted to be treated like an adult. I realized he was not the one to fill that void in my life. This void I felt would have been impossible for any human to fill. As the weekend dragged on, I realized I had changed too much to go back to what once was or could have been. How pathetic was that? It wasn't even that good in the first place, so why did I want to go back? I left Chicago actually longing to return to Wichita. Randy may not have been in love with me at the time, but at least by now I did have a job that I enjoyed, and they liked my work ethic. It was a receptionist job at an office supply business. It brought some joy to my wretched life.

If the truth were to be told, one of the motives for going away was to provoke Randy to jealousy, to try to make him want me more than his partying life. I was longing for him to desire me, pull me close to him, and make me whole. I was optimistic that he missed me and would rush to me and tell me how wrong his behavior had been. On the plane, I prayed it would be different, anything, just not the same.

I came back to the same. All hope vanished. Life was always going to be miserable. Randy picked me up at the airport and treated me as if I had not even been gone. He struggled with asking me about my weekend. I asked him about his. He had partied the weekend away with people at work. He did not say much, but I knew he felt guilty. I left it at that, and we went on as usual.

Within six weeks Randy called me up at work to tell me he had been promoted to assistant buyer and needed to be in Ft. Worth in a couple of days. Unlike the previous move, this time I *wanted* to move. I liked Texas. I hated our life in Wichita, and with our relationship in crisis, I was ready for the change. It was easier for me to blame the city of Wichita and not our sinful behavior. My only regret was leaving my friend Lori, who had become like a sister to me.

Randy left immediately. (Little did I know the Lord was beginning to answer my prayers on the plane that day.) This move would become the beginning of many changes. I stayed behind a little over a week to fulfill my notice at work and to tighten up some loose ends. For Randy, this was a great career move. He was excited about being a buyer for the stores and getting to go to New York a couple of times a year. He saw it as a chance to start again, a new venture.

When I arrived in Ft. Worth, Randy acted as if he was actually glad to see me. I was shocked and a little suspicious. I really did not know what to think of him anymore; I was wounded from the past, and I did not trust his newfound affection for me. Over a period of time, it appeared that Randy was becoming more considerate toward me. He began to share with me the conversations he was hearing at work. The majority of his colleagues were women. He had begun to sit and really listen to their discussions. Some of these conversations were about how great their husbands were. Then others would complain about what their husbands did not do. He started to take notice of his behavior toward me. For me it was already too late. Two and a half years of bad treatment was enough for me. I was letting bitterness and resentment rise up in my heart toward him. I had been hurt so many times that I did not know what to think of him anymore.

However, I did heed Randy's advice and attempted college again. I took six hours at the local junior college. To my surprise, this time I did rather well. This was stunning, given my grades in high school! My mind quickly became consumed with school. It became my god. Soon, all I wanted was an education.

The marriage was a little better. Let us just say that for the first time in years, Randy and I began to "click" as a couple. We spent a bit more time with each other. When we did go out, it was with other couples. Life was a tad better than it had been in the past.

My relationship with my mother was about the same. Every time I went home for a visit I stayed at my sister's house rather than with my mother. I would see her while I was there, but it wasn't a priority. I always enjoyed the company of young children. When I went home one of my main objectives was to spend time with my nieces and nephews.

Even though Randy and I had been married for four years, I was very aware we were not ready for children. School was my priority. Since I was not ready to start a family myself, I decided to volunteer my time. I signed up for "Big Brothers and Big Sisters," a federal program for helping kids at risk. I filled out the paperwork, and within three months I had become Heidi's "Big Sister." I enjoyed Heidi. Randy and I did activities with her. We took her to the movies, bowling, and occasionally we played miniature golf.

In a subtle way, being a volunteer was changing me. I finally accepted the fact that I never would have the mother-daughter relationship I sought after with my own mother, but I realized that I could have a close relationship with someone else. It was important for me to give to others what I was missing. I never liked to see children hurting the way I did as a child. Spending time with Heidi was good for me; I got my mind off myself and onto her. I believed that if I kept myself busy, then I would not have to look inward. A good defense mechanism, don't you think?

I wanted to go to school full-time, but with my present job, it just was not possible. I happened to meet a girl at school who worked for an attorney who needed a receptionist for his title company. I applied and got the job. This job was flexible. They would allow me to take morning classes and work thirty hours a week: a perfect fit.

Meanwhile, Randy was having an epiphany and I did not even notice. He was beginning to examine himself and become more introspective. He did not like what he saw. He began reading books on the "inner soul." He read one, in particular, on "personality." It was not a book of faith; nevertheless, it seemed to help him. He realized that his father had struggled with experiencing and showing his emotions, just as Randy did. Randy realized how jealous he had been of his older brother as they were growing up. He was compelled to call his brother and apologize. Unfortunately, his brother was not responsive, but Randy felt released from a burden of guilt. He even called his mother to share about his conversation with his brother and his epiphany. His mother was thrilled. After this, their relationship became very strong. For the first time she was able to have conversations about "feelings" with Randy. He was making progress.

Oddly enough, as he was opening up, I was shutting down. Although he no longer spoke down to me, I was drifting away. I had given so much to this relationship and never felt as though I was getting anything back. I wanted to leave him several times, yet I had nowhere to go. Therefore, I stayed.

Even though I was working thirty hours a week, we did not have enough money to pay for my school. Randy took a second job to help make ends meet. He became a telemarketer, selling newspapers, and roofing for homes, at night. This cold calling in the evening made Randy consider changing careers. He had been working at Dillard's for four years now, and yet here he was having to work a second job just to make ends meet. He felt his career was stagnating.

Since he was busy working all the time, school became everything to me. I began to think that education was the answer for every social woe. I knew how it was helping me, and I was convinced it would do the same for others. I was becoming very secular in my thinking. I fell for much of the humanistic doctrine. My search for knowledge blinded me to sin. I idolized my professors because of their education. I was a prime candidate for indoctrination.

A professor at school took a liking to me. He began to speak to me in the hall outside of class. He would walk me down the hall. I loved chatting with him. He was a gifted teacher who made his subject come alive. We began to discuss many social issues and of course, politics. At the time, Randy did not like to discuss anything but sports and work, so I was taken to this man. He treated me like a woman with an intellect. The attention he gave me was flattering; I thoroughly enjoyed the discourse. It stimulated my mind. He saw me as more than just a pretty face. Soon, I was deceived. Unfortunately, this relationship went further than it should have gone. It saddens me to think of the state I was in, falling for another man just because he paid attention to me. I was just too needy at the time.

Randy was rapidly losing interest in the retail business. On one of our trips back home, Randy happened to mention his frustration with his job to his father. His father mentioned that Antone, the town broker, was looking for a partner. He immediately inquired about the position. Antone had Randy come in and visit. Antone was very interested in Randy, but he did not have the authority to make the final decision. Randy would have to interview with the home office in Milwaukee. A new enthusiasm arose in Randy. He was sure the brokerage business was the career he wanted to pursue.

We went back home and Randy anxiously waited for the brokerage interview. About two weeks after we returned home, Randy was off to Milwaukee for his anticipated interview. They put him through the interview of his life. He returned mentally exhausted. Within a week, however, he had the job. For the first time since our very first move to Texas, we were both excited about starting something new. We were clueless of the plans the Lord had for us.

It was a couple of days before Christmas 1987 and once again, we found ourselves in the middle of a move. As it was in Wichita, we could not find a place to live. We stayed with my sister until we were able to move into our home. Within a few days we were able to rent an older home. It had gold shag carpet in the family room and blue shag in the living room. You could say it was a colorful house if you were being nice. It came with a washer and dryer, though, and it was only three blocks from Randy's new office. It was not what I would have chosen, but it was a place to live, and that was a blessing!

In January, I began to attend the local university. Both Randy and I were students; he studied at work to prepare for his license. In order for him to sell stocks and bonds, he had to pass his "series seven" test. Once Randy passed, it was obligatory that he go to Milwaukee for six weeks of training. When he returned, he was a broker. Randy's demeanor began to change; he loved what he was doing and looked forward to the challenge ahead of him. Our relationship began to change as well. He began to share his heart with me. It seemed as if we had a few breakthroughs, and perhaps we were growing up a little.

The Lord began to work on me more than before. Drinking socially began to lose its appeal to me. I was uninterested in the bar scene, bored, and tired of the sin in my life. For the first time in a long time, I wanted a different existence. Uncannily, the same changes were occurring within my sister, and she decided to go back to church. She asked me to come along. I went with her not realizing that the events of that day would change my life forever. As I sat there and listened to the sermon, the Lord spoke to my heart. I could feel His presence. I knew it was time to return home. I felt like a wayward child who had been gone from home for a very long time. At the end of the service, I walked slowly down that aisle with tears running down my face. I was so ashamed of my behavior, and I began to tell God how sorry I was. I got on my knees and asked Him to forgive me. That day I told Him how much I loved Him, and how I wanted Him to be my Lord. All that sin that had entangled my life lifted off that day. Through every tear, I could feel His cleansing power. I wanted no part of the life I was leading; I left it at the door. I simply wanted nothing to do with it anymore. The joy I found that day was what I had been searching for. My experience is not an anomaly. Many people have felt the touch of the Lord. The Word speaks so eloquently of what a heart feels after the hand of the Lord touches a soul.

My lips will shout for joy when I sing praises to You;
And my soul, which You have redeemed.
My tongue also will utter Your righteousness all day long;
For they are ashamed, for they are humiliated
who seek my hurt.

Psalm 71:23-24 (NASU)

While I was at the altar pouring my heart out to God, Randy was watching from the back of the church. He was curious about what was taking place. He wondered, "Why is she crying?" He had never felt the Lord before. Even though we attended church as a couple, it was more as an obligation than a celebration. The conviction of the Holy Spirit was something one rarely felt in the church we attended. During all the years prior to that day, we had walked out of church just as lost as when we had walked in.

That day felt almost celestial; I felt as though I was floating in the air. I felt like I had taken the longest spiritual bath in history. My heart was squeaky clean. I knew I had been forgiven. Randy saw a sparkle in me that was not there before, yet he still wasn't convinced this "Jesus thing" was for him. He still attended his church as well as the one I was attending. He went and spoke to his priest about different perceptions he was experiencing. He was searching, and God was about ready to do something spectacular.

My church was planning an upcoming revival, and I wanted to go each night. Randy was embarrassed to attend when he saw the word "revival" on the marquee, but he went reluctantly anyway. That very night during the revival, he gave his heart to the Lord. At the altar, the Holy Spirit was touching him; I could see the tears streaming down his face, and he was truly being changed. The beautiful hand of the Lord was at work, busy cleansing. The Lord's work opened him up emotionally. There was such a change in him. Randy became sweeter, kinder, and more affectionate. The chains that had bound him for so long came off that night at the altar. He had been set free from an emotionless state and was able to express his feelings. Not only did God do a work that night for Randy's sake, but also He blessed me with a wonderful husband. That night my life changed forever.

Now, being married as a Christian is so much more adventurous than being married as a non-Christian, and it makes for a much better story, which brings us to a completely new chapter in my life.

CHAPTER FIVE

Marriage, A.D.

Therefore if any person is [ingrafted] in Christ (the
Messiah) he is a new creation (a new creature altogether);
the old [previous moral and spiritual condition] has passed
away. Behold, the fresh and new has come!

2 Corinthians 5:17 (AMP)

W hen I think back on our early years of marriage
"before Christ" and then "after Christ," it amazes me
what a little time with Christ can do. When we came to know
Christ, life was enhanced like never before. For the first time,
life seemed enchanting. It is so hard to explain the difference
in both of us. Randy and I actually began to fall in love with
one another. I mean, we *cherished* our time together. Just as
the scripture says, we were literally "new creatures." It was
as though God shone the Light on us and we were finally
able to see clearly. We were in a Bible-based church where
the Word of God was preached with passion. God began to
direct our paths. We began to pay our tithes, something we
had never done before. Randy's salary climbed so much that
we were actually able to pay our bills and even save a little.

This in itself was a miracle, because in the past we could barely make ends meet.

Praying together became a common practice. We were excited about helping in our church. I taught children's church and Randy taught a "Promise Keepers" class to the men.

I could hardly believe it, but life was finally worth living. Randy loved his job, and I was doing well in school. I was just about to graduate with that long-sought-after Bachelor's Degree. In addition, I understood the place of education at last! Education is great and it can help alleviate many financial woes, but it cannot fill the void that God has placed in every heart. The emptiness in a heart is made exclusively for the Lord, and nothing else can fill it, not even a long-sought-after desire like education. My educational accomplishments gave me only temporary self-esteem, but over the years, God has revealed to me that my self-esteem comes from who I am in Him! Finally, I "get" this Christianity thing!

I was just about finished with college, and we were thinking very seriously about starting a family. We had been married six years now, and we felt like it was time. I was twenty-six and Randy was twenty-eight. We were settled enough in our lives that we knew we were together forever. From the beginning of our marriage, we had always agreed that we wanted a house full of children. I think our love for children was a major attraction for the both of us. Randy and I were both from a family of six children.

Unbeknownst to Randy, I began to pray for a baby or two. In my prayer closet, I asked God for a set of twins. I even prayed for identical twin girls. I remember my prayer: "Lord I would love to have identical twins; if You think I can handle it, would You please bless me with this request?"

We tried for seven or eight months to conceive. Then one day we got word. I was finally pregnant; God had answered my prayer. This was March of 1990, and by April 1, I was not feeling well at all. You have heard of morning sickness.

Forget the morning; I was sick morning, noon, and night! The only time I did feel good was when I was sleeping! Unfortunately, sleep only came between bathroom breaks.

This pregnancy was not fun. I was definitely not one of those "glowing pregnant women," the type that look cute and love being pregnant. No, I gained an excessive amount of weight; and my face had become so full. I asked the doctor, "Am I going to get stretch marks on my face?" He chuckled and said, "I haven't seen that one yet."

Pregnancy was difficult for me in more ways than just being sick. I have always had an excessive amount of energy, and being pregnant forced me to rest more. Since I am so high strung, I struggled with wondering if I was just being lazy. However, when I found out the news during my fourth month that I was not only pregnant with one, but *two* babies, this helped me realize that my extreme "morning" sickness and tiredness were both warranted! I was overjoyed. God gave me my heart's desire!

Then in my seventh month, my excessive joy was superseded with fear. I became preeclamptic (excessive fluid in the amniotic sac, which causes high blood pressure). Because of the preeclampsia and a leaking membrane, I went into premature labor. My twins were born 5 ½ weeks early. Since the girls were early, we feared their lungs had not had time to develop. By the end of the day our fears had become reality. Ashley had to be rushed to a larger facility with a neonatal unit. One of her lungs had collapsed. She was life-flighted to Kansas City (it was a hundred miles from the birth hospital). I did not even get to hold her for ten days; this was very disheartening for me. However, Amanda was fine, but her sucking ability had not yet developed so she had to be tube fed.

I knew the Lord had given me these twins and that Satan was trying to rob me of this blessing. Even though I was very sick, I was more concerned with what was going on with my babies. Just a few hours after my delivery, which was by C-section, I started to move around. I looked down at my stomach and realized I was lying in a pool of blood. I called for the nurse. She rushed in the room, jumped on my bed, and put pressure on my abdomen trying to get it to stop bleeding. She rode that gurney, putting pressure on all the way, until we reached surgery. I am thankful for her dedication to her job!

After the surgery, the doctor came in to tell me how sick I was. He informed me that I had Disseminated Intravascular Coagulation (DIC): a bleeding and clotting disorder. He was able to get it under control, but I was not out of danger. The nurses padded my bed and did not want me to move. I was to lie in bed for three days. I was in a lot of pain. I'd had two major surgeries in the same area within a matter of hours. My incision was black and blue, and since my loss of blood was extensive, the doctor was worried I might bleed to death. He also warned me that I might be susceptible to seizures. He gave me preventive medicine to thwart it. This was the 1990s, and many in the medical profession no longer trusted the blood supply. My doctor decided against a blood transfusion unless he had no other alternative. I am thankful he made that decision, even though recovery was slow. It took me a couple of months to build my blood back up, but it was possible with a diet high in iron and protein.

Once the doctor felt I was strong enough to go to the restroom by myself, I was sent home (plus, my insurance did not want to pay anymore.) I had gone into the hospital to deliver two beautiful babies, yet came home empty-handed. My homecoming was bittersweet. I fought off depression by praying a lot. My weakened condition did not help my moods, either.

After I left the hospital it would be another eight days before the girls could come home. Amanda had to stay in the hospital until she could take a bottle. Ashley was doing much better, so she was transferred back to the hospital of her birth, but she too had to stay there until she was able to suck from a bottle. I went up there every day for about four hours and would sit and hold them. I still was very weak, and it took all my energy to do this, but of course it was worth it.

Finally, homecoming day arrived. God in his mercy allowed Randy and me to bring both twins home on the same day. I soon realized that it had been for the best that the twins had a prolonged stay in the hospital. I was too weak that first week I was home to take care of them. I am so glad we persevered.

This trial was one of the greatest of our life together. When we came to Christ, we were not promised that we would not have difficulties, but instead we were promised that when we do, He would see us through them. All Randy and I could do was to hold onto each other and to our relationship with God. We prayed like never before, and a peace came over us that everything was going to be all right.

Interestingly, at the hospital the Lord brought to my mind a scenario that did not make sense to me at the time. About two years prior, I had a prophetic word spoken over me by a prophet who was visiting our church. He said, "I don't want you to fear; everything is going to be all right. You and your children are going to be fine. You will live."

I did not understand this at first. I wondered if he had me mistaken for someone else. I did not have any children at the time, so I just simply disregarded it and went on with my life. Now I realized how true this prophecy had been!

During my stay in the hospital, my mother tried to help. She was there by my side, and yes, she was very worried. As I recall, she did not know what to say or how to encourage me. She was mostly quiet. I believe she was struggling in her own faith. Now that I understand, I know she struggled with who she was in Christ; and thus she was full of fear. Her fears spoke loudly to her. She lived in worry and dread. Never understanding the impact these fears were having on her life, her worries consumed her. Her mood was usually glum. Perhaps this was due in part to her medication. It is so sad that my mother and I never had a conversation that dealt with these issues, or even one in which we apologized to one another. When I think about her, she never mentioned her contribution to our past struggles or acted as if she did much wrong. It must have been too hard for her to look inward. Occasionally subjects from the past came up; her first response was to blame my father for everything. Maybe this is partly true. Yet, it is sad that there was such a lack of communication about our past as a family. Nothing could ever be healed, because it could never be discussed.

Little did I know that because of no open discussion, I was a walking time bomb, full of poison. Ignoring what took place in my childhood seemed to be the best remedy for all the pain of it; "stuffing it" was our family trait, and I had learned it well. I know I always thought that if I ignored it, the pain would go away. Therefore, I went on with my life. I wanted to be a good mother, and I just wanted to take care of my children without dealing with those problems of the past. I became focused on my family. At the time I did not know this would eventually affect my mothering skills. I was in a sea of bondage, and I did not even know how deep the water was.

Life was eventful with twins! Randy and I were so proud of these girls! They made us rich with joy. We were busy, but a delightful sort of busy. God had graced us. I am amazed at how we handled those tiring days! I can look back and realize this was one of the happiest seasons of my life. I had a husband who loved the Lord, twin baby girls, I had my degree, and we were even able to buy our first home. God had given me everything I had desired as a child.

My dreams were becoming a reality. He allowed me to stay home with my children. I was so thankful. I could not believe that He still could bless me so greatly, considering my sinful past. God was revealing His heart to me. It seemed as if understanding God as my heavenly Father became easy once I had my own children. I understood love in a way I was never capable of understanding before. I wanted nothing but the absolute best for my girls; suddenly I realized that this is what God desires for me. He is the giver of all good gifts! My eyes were beginning to open to "Abba," Father, the true heart of God. Two years later, we had a son. That too, was an answer to prayer. I desired a son so desperately, and He gave me the sweetest boy, whom we named Andrew. Andrew and I have been close since the day of his birth. God again blessed me beyond measure. Our family was growing and growing fast. Within two years we were a family of five.

Then within another two years, we were a family of six. We had Alison, our baby. She is the sunshine of our lives; however, those days were set on survival mode. At that point, we had four children under five years old! Our life consisted of dirty diapers, crayons, and "Barney." Those days were hectic but complete! We were younger and had lots of energy to keep up with the crew. Definitely, life was never boring!

With all this business, Randy and I craved some time alone. Then one day we got our chance. We were invited to attend a marriage retreat. Think of it: a whole weekend alone! We were on it! After finding someone to watch all the children, we were off, anticipating the Lord to do great things. We were not disappointed.

At this retreat, the Lord revealed to Randy and me that we needed to deal with our early relationship. At that time in our lives, we had never discussed past actions toward each other. Now it was God's timing. When the timing is right for God to make you "whole," He will force you to deal with whatever is stifling you. He knew that we both carried secret sins. God was going to perform a soul washing, and it began with our need to confess to one another. God wanted to shed light on our darkness.

When sin is exposed to the light, its power is broken. If Satan, who lives in darkness, can keep your sin hidden, then he has power over you and God cannot do what He does best: restoration. The Lord tells in His word what he must do to your hidden sin:

Our iniquities, our secret heart and its
sins [which we would so like to conceal even from
ourselves], You have set in the [revealing] light
of Your countenance.

Psalm 90:8 (AMP)

This revealing light of His countenance meant that God desired for Randy and me to be honest with each another. Though it was extremely hard for me to deal with those past feelings, there had to be communication about the past. It was so easy to ignore the old, ugly feelings. Yet, I knew I had to go with the Spirit of God. When I first talked this out with Randy, it felt good to release all the shame, but it was only temporary relief. In reality, uncorking my bottle of emotions meant I started reliving all the anger that had welled up in me for many years, and I sank into a deep depression. I began to lose weight and I could not sleep. The devil was having a party in my mind. He began to tell me how worthless I was. I wanted to walk away from everything so much so that I even wanted to leave Randy and my adult life behind. The pain became so intense, I felt as though I could not get any relief. Nonetheless, even though I felt like leaving, I would not. I loved my children too much to see them grow up as I did. At the time, I did not know how to fight back spiritually. I did not have enough Scriptures memorized. My sword needed some sharpening.

The Bible teaches us to fight Satan by using the Word only, but I did not know that I could have said, "It is written…" So instead, I fell prey to the lies of the devil. My life became full of fear, and my faith was shaken. I could not get past my pain to see that God was moving on my behalf. I had to deal with the past so He could take me deeper. This was the process God used to heal me. Then I would be able to fulfill my call and minister to others. Unfortunately, it took longer than it should have, because I fell into the trap of condemnation. Satan got a foothold in my spirit and I lived in misery for approximately six months. It was pitiful. I tried to resist the devil in my own power and failed miserably. Instead of finding healing and relief, I was tormented about my self worth. Satan constantly told me how ugly I was and that I was a failure at everything. I felt as though I was in utter darkness. It was a hint of what my mother had faced every day.

I even sought professional counseling and that seemed to help a little. The counselor opened my eyes to my behavior, and that it was mostly reactions to a wounded spirit. I began to understand that many of my extended family's arguments were due to their wounded spirits, also. Jesus exposed the bondage I was in, and that I was carrying it around like an "old friendly" backpack. God used the counseling to identify and name the problems, but my healing was God's work alone. He would not let me lie in my self-pity any longer. He peeled my soul back like an onion, layer by layer. Finally, He forced me to deal with it once and for all.

For the first time I started to realize the harm that my own sin had caused. I knew about the harm that everyone else's sin had caused in my life, but I was blinded to my own. The light of God was shining into my darkness. I came to understand that the Word of God is the handbook of life, not just platitudes of dos and don'ts, but a personal love letter written to me. It is a beautiful letter written to guide His children through life. Suddenly, I understood God at a deeper level.

With this insight, my healing began on the weekend of the marriage retreat. Please notice the word "began." Actually, this healing took nine long years. He gave me those first five years as a new Christian to strengthen my walk. Although God knew I needed major "heart surgery," I was not ready until that marriage retreat. He also knew how much I loved my children and how determined I was to see them grow up in the best possible home. I was not going to repeat the mistakes of my past. I was determined to make this marriage and my life work. When God saved me, He was taking me on a path of restoration. However, in order for that process to begin, I had to deal with the stuff in my past and present: I had to forgive Randy just as God had forgiven me, and then push forward.

I was letting my emotions control my life. God wanted me to deal with the past, and I finally recognized that even my emotions must come under the authority of the Lord. What is so bizarre about this mess is the paradox: I was too emotional and Randy was not emotional enough! No one in his or her right mind would have put Randy and me together in marriage, let alone expected us to stay together! However, God knew how Randy and I would develop under His guidance. He saw the end from the beginning.

Today Randy is not the same man I married. He has become an affectionate husband and wonderful father, and all my friends are crazy about him. He is the most generous, compassionate, funny, and tenderhearted man I know. I am just enamored with him. God has made an unbelievable change in Randy's life. It is hard to remember the time when he was emotionally bound, when any expression of sadness or real display of emotion was out of the question. When Christ came into his life, these chains were broken. Now, He is free from his insecurities and able to reveal his real heart, because Christ has given him confidence. This transformation has truly been amazing. I am so thankful that not only did God set Randy free, but also He gave me the husband I always wanted. Not only that, but Randy truly loves me. He now expresses his love towards me all the time.

Since we came to Christ, our life has been an adventure, full of surprises. After twenty-three years of marriage, I am honestly astounded at the life we have together. I know I do not deserve God's blessings, but He still gives them out in abundance.

The greatest of all blessings is that my children are reaping the benefits of parents who have dealt with their past. Our children know that we love one another and we are in this marriage for life. We want them to understand the value of family and how priceless each one of them is to us. We hug our children and encourage them. All of them are active in school, church, and sports. This is the complete opposite of how I was raised. However, if it were not for the Lord, my life would still be broken. My children's lives would be broken, and probably their children's lives would be as well. All my siblings have been divorced at least once and this has affected their children. In my extended family, many of my nieces and nephews are suffering from the same sins as my parents. Many of them have struggled with substance abuse and have problems keeping a job. Sadly, I even have a twenty-three year old nephew in prison. These destructive behaviors could have gone on and on, but in my immediate family it stopped here with Randy and me! With Jesus in the equation, you can beat the odds.

Now we are building a Godly heritage for generations and generations to come. In this house, we pray together. We discuss things and try to seek God's perspective on our decisions. We read the Word daily; this has been our children's life since birth. It is awesome when I walk into my children's rooms at night and they too are reading the Word. We teach them to seek God on their own. Sometimes when they ask me if they can go somewhere that I am not sure they should go, I encourage them to pray about it. We want them to know that God desires to speak with them as well as with us.

God restored my marriage. He has given my children the family I longed for. He surprises me with His gifts of restoration and grace. I love Him more and more each day. His thumbprint is all over my life. I know where I would be if He had not intervened. Although my life is far from perfect, I now have a peace that was never there before. Although I still have many trials, I have learned to rest in Him. I know He will take care of me, because I am His child, just like my children can rest with me, knowing I will always be there for them when they need me.

After Randy and I overcame the marriage hurdle in our lives, we were hit again. In October of 1997, my mother was driving to my sister's house when she lost control of her vehicle for a moment and hit a parked car. As soon as we heard the news, we rushed to the hospital. She seemed fine, though a little shaken. The doctor decided to keep her overnight, and within forty-eight hours her prognosis changed dramatically. The next thing I knew she was in Intensive Care with Adult Respiratory Distress Syndrome, a mostly fatal respiratory problem. They had to put her on a respirator. She stabilized and we did not see any change for a couple of weeks. My older sister, Della, wanted her transferred to a large hospital, and everyone agreed. We followed her up to KU Medical Center. She was there a little over a week. It was like a scene from the past, just like when my father died. As she was fighting the inevitable death, my siblings and I gave her permission to die. We told her that it was all right to go home. The Lord was waiting with a far better life for her.

It was sad that her life was over, but I could not bring myself to cry. Similar to how I felt when my father died, I was unable to mourn my mother's death because there had never been a true relationship between us. I believe I was more relieved than sad. She had worried so much in her lifetime, and had constantly struggled with feeling defeated, that I found myself comforted to know that her unhappy life was over. She had been a Christian, so I had peace knowing she was in Heaven for eternity. And I am forever grateful to the Lord that we all had time to tell her our goodbyes.

So now both of my parents were deceased. Being their daughter was over. Even though they were in Heaven with the Lord, I still felt pain from my childhood. I never shared anything about the past with anyone. I covered my pain well, but God had done a miracle in my marriage, and now He was going to work on my broken heart from my childhood. At this point I was in my thirties, and over the years I had formed many layers of protection that God was going to have to peel away, just like in my relationship with Randy. I should have known God was not going to let me keep my resentment. He gave me a few years after my mother's death, and then He said it was time to deal with that bitterness in my heart. God began to deal with one layer at a time. I will end Part I of this book with the following passage of Scripture; it became my heart's prayer during the next season of my life. It was time to purify my heart.

Create in me a pure heart, O God,
and renew a steadfast spirit within me.
Do not cast me from your presence
or take your Holy Spirit from me.
Restore to me the joy of your salvation
and grant me a willing spirit, to sustain me.
Then I will teach transgressors your ways,
and sinners will turn back to you.
Save me from bloodguilt, O God,
the God who saves me,
and my tongue will sing of your righteousness.

Psalm 51:10-14 (NIV)

My father

My mother

My wedding

My wonderful family

PART TWO

BOOT CAMP TIME

The Process of Breaking Free
From My Own Prison

CHAPTER SIX

The Fruits of Bitterness: My Own Prison

You have no part or share in this ministry, because your heart is not right before God. Repent of this wickedness and pray to the Lord. Perhaps he will forgive you for having such a thought in your heart. For I see that you are full of bitterness and captive to sin.

Acts 8:21-23 (NIV)

Has an apple ever been so appealing to your eye that your mouth began to salivate before you even took that first bite? It is red and shiny and you cannot wait to sink your teeth into it! Imagine that finally you take that long-anticipated bite, but it is not what you expected. There is bitterness inside the bright shiny apple. And imagine that it not only tastes bitter, but a worm has worked his way through that apple! What a disappointment! Unfortunately, for quite some time this is precisely how my life could have been described. On the outside I looked bright and shiny. I acted as if I had it all together. But you know, looks can be deceiving, and I was the master of disguise. Even after I became a Christian,

I never let people know about the hurt that so deeply undermined my life. I had a worm eating away at my heart.

In Webster's dictionary the word *bitter* is defined as "having or being a taste that is sharp, acrid, and unpleasant. (2) Causing sharp physical or mental pain or discomfort: Harsh (3) Difficult or distasteful to accept, admit, or bear."[1] This was the very definition of my personality.

A part of me was bitter, unpleasant, and harsh. The seeds of bitterness had been sown in my life for many years, long ago. Now the fruit of bitterness was bringing forth a harvest, and I had no idea that I was actually cultivating it! I was judgmental, self-righteous, and unhappy. I had fooled myself into thinking that since I was a Christian, I had dealt with my past, while in reality all I did was ignore it and consider it to be "behind me." I guess that is what a prideful spirit will do for you!

I knew I did not like myself, but I did not understand why. I had been rejected most of my life by people who were supposed to love me. This rejection affected me to the core of my being. When you are in a rejected state of mind, it is impossible to realize just how self-absorbed you have become.

By this time in my life I had been a Christian for many years, yet I still had fits of anger, talked about people behind their backs, and was negative and judgmental. Often, I showed no compassion at all. This is the picture of a carnal Christian. In Galatians 3:3 Paul asks, "Are you so foolish? After beginning with the Spirit, are you now trying to attain your goal by human effort?" (NIV) If I knew someone was struggling with a certain sin, I might tell him or her a story or quote a scripture that had to do with his or her sin problem; I was abrupt and frank. I wanted them to see the error of their ways. At times, I was downright mean. I guess I thought the Holy Spirit needed my help to do His job! It is good to remember what the Scriptures tell us about this particular subject.

> Or how can you say to your brother,
> 'Brother, let me take out the speck that is in your eye,'
> when you yourself do not see the log that is in your
> own eye? You hypocrite, first take the log out of your
> own eye, and then you will see clearly to take out the
> speck that is in your brother's eye.

> Luke 6:42-43 (NASU)

Can you see just how the bitterness in my life was a result of the fact that I myself was wounded? Not only did I exhibit this atrocious behavior, but I also expected others to make me happy, and when they did not, I was disappointed in them.

What a mess I was, and on top of all this, I had a horrible temper! I would get very angry and blow up as fast as a whistle on a teakettle! If the children did something minor, I could scream and yell for two minutes straight about nothing, rambling on like a fool. It was as though I had lost my mind for a moment. This did not modify their behavior at all; in fact, all it did was scare them. I remember the twins, when they were little, looking at me with frightened eyes as though they feared me. What a terrible thing for anyone to experience, especially two adorable toddlers!

Once my "fit" was over, I would feel terrible, and then condemnation would set in. Within minutes I would have to go apologize for my horrible behavior. It was a cycle of sin, repent, sin some more, repent, sin some more, and on and on. I would pray and beg God to heal me of this awful behavior. What a miserable way to live!

Nonetheless, I continued in my bondage, walking in the flesh daily. I had my opinions about everything and everyone.

If it were someone I did not know very well, I would cut him or her some slack and not have much to say. However, if it was someone I knew well, or a family member, I let my views be known on whatever he or she did! For example, when my younger sister, who has struggled with drug addictions, would fall from grace, I would judge her to high heaven. I would think to myself, "Why can't she just stop? What is wrong with her?" Then I would get so angry with her and how she treated her children. I would recall the hurt that I had gone through as a child, and I hated to see her make the same mistakes with her own children. It was hard for me to watch my nieces and nephews hurting. She was repeating the horrible habits of my father. I would have talks with her, hoping to give her "spiritual" advice, but she was in darkness, and could not act on this "advice" because she did not know Christ. It was as if I was clueless as to how to be effective as a Christian.

I thought my attitude toward my sister was right and that all the problems were hers, until I came across what Christ had to say about my judgmental attitude. When I read the following scripture, my blood ran cold:

> "For in the same way you judge others,
> you will be judged, and with the measure you use,
> it will be measured to you."
>
> Matthew 7:2 (NIV)

This scripture hit me between the eyes. I knew immediately I needed to repent, thank Him for showing me mercy, and begin showing mercy and love to others. Then I realized that I needed to fall on my face in prayer and ask God to deliver my sister as he had delivered me. I had judged her critically instead of praying God's mercy for her. Oh sisters, if you know someone who has children, and he or she is not walking with the Lord as they should, pray for them as never before! Do this before you even say a word!

The Bible makes it clear that the law of "sowing and reaping" is absolute. We all have to face consequences for our actions. However, sisters, do not judge as I did; instead, pray for each other, remembering that reaping what we have sown is punishment enough for all of us!

I did not get along with my younger sister who did not know the Lord, but neither did I get along with the older ones who did. We fought to the point that we could not carry on a normal conversation. If any one of us made a suggestion to the other, she would get offended and retaliate with sharp words. These vicious cycles went round and round like a ferris wheel in a nightmarish carnival.

What is most disheartening about this kind of behavior is that most of us believe we are behaving as Christians! It is sad when people who love the Lord can't get along because of pride and jealousy. I avoided being around my sisters unless it was obligatory, and then they took offense at that as if I thought I was better than them! This behavior of my sisters and mine continued over the years until the Lord started to deal with my wounded spirit. Finally, during my season of fasting and being in the Word, there was a breakthrough. As I studied His Word, conviction gripped my soul, especially when I read this passage of Scripture:

Let all bitterness and indignation and wrath
(passion, rage, bad temper) and resentment
(anger, animosity) and quarreling (brawling, clamor,
contention) and slander (evil-speaking, abusive or
blasphemous language) be banished from you, with
all malice (spite, ill will, or baseness of any kind).
And become useful and helpful and kind to one another,
tenderhearted (compassionate, understanding,

loving-hearted), forgiving one another [readily and freely],
as God in Christ forgave you.

Ephesians 4:31 – 5:1 (AMP)

Beloved, even though I struggled in many relationships,
I would not see myself as part of the problem; I always
assumed it was the other person who had the problem. My
life was in constant turmoil and drama as I lived in daily fric-
tion. It seemed as though I fed off of arguing with someone,
if not a friend, then a family member (mostly the latter).

What an insane way to live life! Can you imagine what
that does to your mental and emotional state? This is the
fruit of bitterness, right to the core. I am surprised I had any
friends at all! The fact that I did is just proof of the grace of
God!

Unbelievably, during this time, I still went to church three
times a week. I was reading my Bible and really seeking the
Lord. Frustration began to rise up in my heart. I wanted so
much to be different, but I did not know how to go about it. I
would plead with God to help me overcome my argumenta-
tive lifestyle.

Though frustrated, I knew God had not forsaken me. In
my cries out to Him, He was healing me; it was just taking
longer than I expected. I did not understand the process
called "sanctification." When God led me to quit my job,
I began studying His Word like never before. Actually, He
was transforming my mind through His Word.

Do not be conformed to this world (this age),
[fashioned after and adapted to its external, superficial
customs], but be transformed
(changed) by the [entire] renewal of your mind
by its new ideals and its new attitude], so that you may
prove [for yourselves] what is the good and

acceptable and perfect will of God, even the thing which is good and acceptable and perfect [in His sight for you].

Romans 12:2 (AMP)

He was rebirthing me through His Word. He was cleansing me. There had been so much junk poured into my life for so long that I was in a state of complete bewilderment. My parents had always dealt with things in an irrational way. My mother would just throw fits, and my father would sulk or leave; they never discussed difficult situations. Depending on the situation, I found myself being just as irrational as my parents had been. It was unpredictable, though. One day I might sulk, and on another day I might blow up. Thank God, He does not let us stay where we are if we really seek Him! He loves us too much!

When God started dealing with my sin and bad behavior, He did it in such a loving way. I never felt that He was pointing a finger at me to hurt me or shame me, but only to help me. He showed me the errors of my ways so He could restore me. He showed me He loved me regardless of my behavior, and that He has great plans for me. Nevertheless, He also showed me that unless I allowed Him to heal me, He would not be able to use me the way He intended. Once this dawned on me, I repented immediately for my past behavior, and a new attitude began to develop in my heart. This led to the best mental health I have ever experienced. My life is no longer a soap opera, and everyone in my house is a lot happier because mama is happier!

I love the following scriptures, because in order for God to heal me I had to get serious enough to allow Him to search my inward secrets. It was difficult, but it was worth every bit of pain.

Search me, O God, and know my heart;
test me and know my anxious thoughts.
See if there is any offensive way in me,
and lead me in the way everlasting.

Psalm 139:23-24 (NIV)

Beloved, can you see what my bondage did to me? It suppressed me from being what Christ had called me to be. This bondage was controlling my life, while at the same time Christ was trying to set me free. I was shattered emotionally. He could not use a legalistic, bitter Christian. I could not be Christ's ambassador unless I represented Him well. Do you know that you are called to be an ambassador, too? Everyone who knows Christ is called to be an ambassador!

We are therefore Christ's ambassadors,
as though God were making his appeal through us.
We implore you on Christ's behalf: Be reconciled to God.
God made him who had no sin to be sin for us,
so that in him we might become
the righteousness of God.

2 Corinthians 5:20-21 (NIV)

There is nothing greater in my life than being used by Christ to affect others' lives. I love to lead others to Him and just love them up! When you look at others, do you see their souls? When the Lord healed me, I realized it was not about me anymore. It was now all about Him. I am now living in a freedom that is the opposite of bitterness.

Ladies, learn from my mistakes: do not hold on to any unforgiveness or bitterness. It is a waste of time. God really did a work in me. I had to forgive, let go, and go on. I have now taken the first step in restoring my relationship with my sisters. I call them more. I take them to lunch and encourage them. The pressure is off me now, and God has to do the rest. I know that I am not to point fingers or find fault. It is God's job to change people, and He can handle it. I instead pray for blessings on my family.

God has graciously brought me to the point where I want to please Him more than I want "my way." When He requires difficult things from me, I know I have to trust Him. I have learned that if I just take action, then my feelings will follow. Anyway, God has a perfect track record. Any sacrifice in the past that He has requested of me has turned out to be beneficial. He is a great boss to work for! Talk about fringe benefits — His are second to none!

CHAPTER SEVEN

What I Learned From Head Lice and Plantar Warts

—⊙ℐ✎—

And after you have suffered a little while, the God of all grace [Who imparts all blessing and favor], Who has called you to His [own] eternal glory in Christ Jesus, will Himself complete and make you what you ought to be, establish and ground you securely, and strengthen, and settle you.

1 Peter 5:10 (AMP)

How many of you have experienced those annoying trials that seem to last an eternity but in reality only last a few months? I want to share with you the wisdom I have gained from a couple of these nuisances in my life: head lice and plantar warts. I do not know how many of you mothers have dealt with head lice, but I have three times! By the time I finished my three-year cycle with head lice, I hoped I would never have to even think about it again. However, if it happens, I know God will give me the grace to get through it, one more time.

> But He said to me, My grace
> (My favor and loving-kindness and mercy) is
> enough for you [sufficient against any danger
> and enables you to bear the
> trouble manfully]; for My strength and power
> are made perfect (fulfilled and completed) and show them-
> selves most effective in [your] weakness.
> Therefore, I will all the more gladly glory in my weak-
> nesses and infirmities, that the strength and power
> of Christ (the Messiah) may rest (yes, may pitch
> a tent over and dwell) upon me!

2 Corinthians 12:9 (AMP)

First let me explain that my twin girls have extremely thick, coarse, and very curly hair. It is so thick that Robyn, their hairdresser, comments about it every single time she cuts and dries it. If you have ever had to deal with head lice in kids, I think you understand what kind of mess head lice can cause in thick, long, curly hair! With two of these kids contracting head lice, I was done in!

This trial came about at one of the busiest times of my life. At the time, my four children were at the ages of six, four and two. I was driving my children to their Christian school, which was 35 miles away from our home. I would drop them off and go to work two days a week at our family store, which was 15 miles away from my home in the opposite direction! Picture this: after going 35 miles to school, I would then turn around and drive 50 miles back to work! We had just remodeled my husband's family's furniture store and were having a "grand re-opening." I was very instrumental in changing the image of the store. It was crucial that I be there. Guess what? Right in middle of this chaos, the twins came home with head lice for the first time! This was double trouble in many ways. I thought only dirty people got head lice. I was horrified that my own babies' heads were now crawling with lice!

As much work as it was to get rid of these nasty parasites, you would think I would have come out of this experience with compassion for any mother who found herself in this position. But no, not me. After round #1 with head lice, all I knew was I never wanted my kids to have it again. Shortly afterward I was helping in the church nursery on a particular Sunday. A precious young mother, who was a first-time visitor to the church, brought her child into the nursery so she could enjoy the service without interruption. As the nursery worker was holding her little baby, we looked carefully and saw the baby had "nits" in his hair. We immediately sent someone to get the mother. She returned to the nursery perplexed. I must confess that I wasn't at all nice. I let fear overcome me, and instead of acting with love, I gave her child back with nothing but frustration. When I think back on my behavior, I am appalled at myself! I was certainly only thinking about myself at the time and not how humiliated that poor mother must have felt. I hope I did not give her a bad taste of Christianity, because I sure wasn't Christ-like that day. Even as I write about this incident, I am still so ashamed of my actions.

> Let no one then seek his own good and
> advantage and profit, but [rather] each one of the
> other [let him seek the welfare of his neighbor].
>
> 1 Corinthians 10:24 (AMP)

What about you? Have you every blown it with others because you were consumed with yourself? If you have, aren't you thankful for God's grace? When we mess things up as I did with this woman, at least we can go to God and come clean. Aren't you grateful?

Let us then fearlessly and confidently and boldly
draw near to the throne of grace
(the throne of God's unmerited favor to us sinners),
that we may receive mercy [for our failures]
and find grace to help in good time for
every need [appropriate help and well-timed help,
coming just when we need it].

Hebrews 4:16 (AMP)

Well, it was obvious from my behavior towards this woman that I had not yet learned my lesson. So wouldn't you know it? The twins contracted head lice again the following year. Of course, it happened at yet another inopportune time. We had moved to a different community so the children could be closer to their school. My son's birthday is right after Christmas. During the first week of January, we had a party for him with lots of new friends. We played "pin the tail on the donkey." Of course, the twins were right in the middle of the action, as always! That evening after the party, I realized the twins had head lice! Now all of our new friends and the whole party had been exposed! Of course, I had to swallow my pride again, call every single parent, and tell him or her, "the twins" might have given their children head lice. Unfortunately, I was so annoyed that I did not ask God, "What are you trying to teach me?" I just went right out and got the paraphernalia to get rid of the lice, one more time. I am certain I spent over $70.00. I vacuumed, sprayed the bedding, washed the sheets, put the stuffed animals in plastic and picked their outrageously thick, long, curly hair for hours at a time. It took at least four or five days, but finally we got rid of the lice.

My lessons with "head lice" were still not complete. As bad as it had been, I had not yet learned humility and compassion. Therefore, the following year those little twins

with the outrageously thick hair contracted lice *again*! I was
starting to think they must have a head-lice gene! If someone
with lice was even in a 5-mile radius of them, they got it.
Now this was getting ridiculous! Nevertheless, what was
most ridiculous is that it took me three episodes of picking
nits to get past the "dirty" stigma and learn compassion for
others in this situation.

It was in May, and we were in the middle of softball
season. I was rushing around trying to get everyone ready
for the game. I was putting their hair up in ponytails to get
it out of the way when I noticed something alive in their
hair. Yes, you guessed it! It was lice. Then in that very split
second I looked at the ceiling and saw water spewing from
the light fixture! The twins' bathroom is right above the foyer.
Quickly, I shut the water off, wiped up the mess, grabbed all
four kids and dashed off to the ball game. I was feeling very
stressed. Anyway, you must be thinking. "She still went to
the ball game?" Oh, yes, with twins there was no option:
they were on the same team, and with the loss of two players
the team would have been disqualified from playing that
night. When we arrived at the ball field, I told each parent
that we found head lice before we came and that absolutely
no one was to share the twins' helmets. After the game, once
again we ran to the store to buy all the paraphernalia. Randy
and I stayed up late and picked through their hair for hours.
Before it was all over, the twins were crying and so were we!
Again, we stripped their beds, sprayed them, vacuumed the
whole house and wiped everything down with bleach. This
time it seemed an impossible task; we did this routine repeatedly. Just when it would appear that we had gotten rid of the
pests, lo and behold, they would return. This went on for
three months. It even became a matter of prayer! Every time
I would check again, there they were. After three months of
praying, cleaning, and working every evening on their hair,
we finally decided to call for a prescription. The prescription

was so harsh that the chemicals actually changed the composition of their hair. However, finally, it worked! The little varmints were dead, and they did not return.

In retrospect, going to the ballgame and explaining to the families that my children had head lice was one more humbling experience. Finally, after this trial, I learned to pray for people with this problem, and not judge them. I could never look down on anyone struggling with head lice again. I just hate that it took three times for me to learn that head lice is not the end of the world.

When Alison, my youngest, contracted head lice, I handled it like a pro. It did not gross me out any longer. I knew exactly what to do, and by this time I had gained some character. In fact, I knew what the enemy was up to, and I was able to get a grip on both the situation and **my emotions**, which was the key.

Do you know that you can pray over your emotions? You can ask God to overcome them, and that is exactly what I did. I had the understanding of who my real enemy was. Just as Thomas Jefferson said, "knowledge is power." The key to overcoming some of the frustration in life is to understand who to be mad at. Channel your energies toward prayer and not your emotions, and speak the Word over your situation. This is the only way to fight our enemy. Sic your big brother Jesus on him! This Scripture is found in Ephesians:

For we are not wrestling with flesh
and blood [contending only with physical opponents],
but against the despotisms, against the powers, against
[the master spirits who are] the world rulers of this present
darkness, against the spirit forces of wickedness in the
heavenly (supernatural) sphere.

Ephesians 6:12 (AMP)

As you can see, my real enemy was not those nasty little varmints, but a wicked spiritual power. God allowed this craziness in my life to mature me. I can tell you, it worked! Ladies, please do not be as obstinate as I was. Learn the first time.

Trials such as this remind me of roller coasters. Imagine you are at an amusement park. Your children talk you into a rollercoaster ride that you know you are going to hate. You get on that ride, praying the whole time you are riding. The prayer goes something like this: "I will never get on this ride again, God, if you just get me off safely." The nightmare is finally over, but then suddenly, you find yourself back in line to ride again! You prayed and struggled, but did not learn your lesson not to do this, so your kids persuade you to ride that horrible rollercoaster one more time. This is what the head lice trial was like for me. Another one of these crazy "rides" came to me in the form of "plantar warts" I hate to admit it, but I had plantar warts for years. I never had a wart until I was pregnant, but after my first pregnancy, I could not seem to get rid of them! They hurt, were embarrassing, and humiliated me if I ever had to show my bare feet. I tried everything to get rid of this nuisance in my life just as I did the head lice, but I could not. I even went to the podiatrist, and he would put an acid solution on those warts. All this accomplished was that I got blisters on my feet and endured a lot of pain. It hurt to walk for a couple of days, but still, I had the warts.

A friend suggested, "Put duct tape on them. Do not let them breathe." I was desperate enough to follow her suggestion unquestioningly, and it worked! Well, at least a few of them disappeared, but a few stubbornly remained. I kept tape on these annoyances day and night. Sometimes I would even scrape away a layer of skin thinking that I could get to the wart itself and kill it! But of course I had no success; I could not get rid of them for the life of me. Finally, I prayed about it. I even spoke healing scriptures over my warts! I asked God to give me divine healing! He did not.

Then another friend, Belinda, was over visiting one time, and I told her about my predicament. She suggested a wart formula from a local pharmacist. I was desperate, so I thought, "Why not?" The tape treatment certainly was not working. I called my doctor and he called in a prescription. Several bottles later, after I had applied it to my warts every day, sometimes twice a day, it finally began to work. The skin began to look different. Layers of skin would peel off one at a time, and then I would re-apply the prescription. It was amazing how well this worked. I truly believe this saved me from surgery or at the very least from the misery of living with warts for the rest of my life.

When they were finally gone, I asked God, "Why didn't you just heal me?" His answer shocked me. He wanted me to learn the healing power of His Word. The Lord told me, "Pam, for Me to heal your wounded heart, you are going to have to apply my Word daily and sometimes even twice a day. I wanted to heal you instantly, but then you would not have understood just how callous you really are and what My Word is capable of doing."

Ladies, God was not telling me just to *read* His Word and believe it; He was saying that I had to apply it, like the medicine. Do you understand the difference? What I read, I had to do. It was a daily process. I learned this wisdom from our heavenly Father because of the plantar warts. Isn't He amazing? He used lice and warts to teach me humility and the power of His Word.

I can now look back on these times with thankfulness. I am glad God changed my heart toward lice, warts, and other things. He showed me in His Word that He is love and compassion, and He was building His own character in me. I wanted to be in the "people business," but in order to get

me there God had some refining to do. This is precisely what
James meant in his epistle:

> Consider it all joy, my brethren, when you encounter
> various trials, knowing that the testing
> of your faith produces endurance.
> And let endurance have its perfect result,
> so that you may be perfect and complete,
> lacking in nothing.
>
> James 1:2-4 (NASU)

Unfortunately, I cannot say I "rejoiced" during my trials,
but I can say that now that these are behind me, I understand
their purposes in my life. Actually, I am thankful for the
lessons learned. God used the simplest things in my life to
help make me more like Him. I wonder what He is using to
try to reach you. Take every frustrating thing that happens to
you and ask Him, "Am I lacking something? What should I
be learning?" If you are lacking in anything, He will develop
that in you, and He can use the circumstances of your life to
teach you His wisdom. I was lacking love and compassion.
He developed it in me. It is so surprising to me how much
I have changed by the power of God's Word, but this was
possible because His Word is real. It can take a heart of stone
and turn it into a heart of flesh.

I believe the Word of God — do you? I have seen it in
action and experienced its power. If you apply it, you too
will see it at work in your life, transforming you! I leave you
with this verse:

> For the word of God is living and active and
> sharper than any two-edged sword, and piercing
> as far as the division of soul and spirit, of both joints
> and marrow, and able to judge the thoughts

and intentions of the heart. And there is
no creature hidden from His sight, but all things
are open and laid bare to the eyes of Him
with whom we have to do.

Hebrews 4:12-13 (NASU)

Jesus is aware of everything that is going on in your life. There is not one thing that is hidden from Him. Ask Him to show you how to be an overcomer. I finally overcame head lice and warts, and gained some wisdom and humility in the process. What stories will He give to you?

If you are struggling within yourself and desire a healing, the next chapter will help you. The power of fasting will take you places that you never thought you could go. Please ask God if you are too callous, full of bitterness, anger, or self-righteousness. If so, there is hope for you. Just swallow your pride, take a big gulp, and keep reading this book. God is going to release you of your misery; I promise you will not be disappointed.

CHAPTER EIGHT

The Power of Fasting in My Life

꘏

When you fast, do not look somber
as the hypocrites do, for they disfigure their faces
to show men they are fasting. I tell you the truth;
they have received their reward in full.

Matthew 6:16 (NIV)

Did you just read that verse? I mean, *really* read it? Jesus said, "*When you fast...*" Did you know that fasting is expected as a normal part of your Christian walk? How many sermons have you heard on fasting lately?

Christ fasted for forty days before He began His ministry! When I had a desire to go into ministry, I should have known He would require this same discipline of me. I myself do not understand what fasting actually accomplishes in the spiritual realm, but it must be a powerful force or Jesus would not have begun His ministry with it. I know that tremendous change came about in my life because of this powerful discipline, and this is what I want to share with you.

First, please recognize that I never really liked to fast. I enjoy eating. In fact, in times prior to this, the most I ever fasted was for forty-eight hours, and even that was a real struggle. I did not quite get it. What could really be accomplished simply by not eating? I was clueless as to the benefits of fasting. I had heard a few sermons calling people to fast and pray. I understood the "prayer" part, but why the "fasting" part? Then again, when I did fast, my motives were more in the flesh, and less in the spirit. I would abstain from food, but I would not feed my spirit with the Word or pray. It was just another obligation. All this was about to change.

In the spring of 2004, God began calling me to fast. Now it had been a year, probably, since my last fast. I do not know why, but suddenly I began feeling compelled to fast. I was contemplating quitting my job, and I wanted God's perfect will in my life. I needed to know if He was leading me into women's ministry or if I was to continue in my teaching job. As I began this fast, I heard the Lord say, "You need to fast for three days."

You might be wondering how I knew it was the Lord speaking to me. Are you kidding? No way would I have ever come up with a three-day fast! I was shell-shocked about taking on a three-day fast. I asked the Lord, "What, really? You do not mean three whole days. Lord, did I hear You correctly? Are You sure You want me to go three days?" Half-heartedly, I obeyed. I said, "Okay, I will fast three days, but You are going to have to help me." I was glad to get through the first day with a minimum of difficulty. I did have a head-ache and I thought my stomach would never stop growling and groaning. Nevertheless, I knew I needed to do this, so I fought back with prayer.

Then I got into the second day, and it was a little easier to say no to my stomach's desires. After forty-eight hours, it became easier than I thought, much to my surprise! In fact, I probably could have gone a little longer than seventy-two hours without food. I did drink water and juice. During this time, I began to really seek God and read His Word. Every time I was tempted to eat, I would pray and recite Scripture, and the pain of hunger would cease. There was a direct correlation between the two. God was feeding my spirit while my flesh was being starved, when usually it had been the other way around.

After I finished the three-day fast, I felt a little different from who I was before. I had such clarity in my life for the first time. I could see God directing my path. I knew things had been changed in me spiritually. My spirit was telling me to quit my job, stay home, and study the Word of God. I believe the fast cleared some of the confusion in my life, and I was able to hear His voice. I truly felt that God was leading me into women's ministry. Teaching the Word became a desire, but I did not know when or how that door was going to open. This was April of 2004. In June of that year I heard the Spirit of God tell me to fast again for three days. I obeyed. It was not as easy as it had been previously. This time, I knew I was fasting for a specific reason, but at the time, I could not grasp the whole picture.

Then He began to request fasting of me on a regular basis. Actually, it was becoming part of my walk with the Lord. I assumed He was guiding and testing my obedience level. Finally, the big request came: He asked me to fast for a week! I was a little hesitant on that one. I thought to myself, "How can I go that long?" "Won't I starve?" "Are you sure you mean a week?"

I thought a bit about the health issues and what no food for a week might do to my body. In addition, I have a husband and four children that I cook for daily. At first I thought this might be too much temptation for me to handle. Nevertheless, God intervened again, and I had a special grace come upon me. I was not nearly as hungry as I anticipated being, and I began to understand that God could (and would) equip me for whatever He was requesting me to do.

I have strength for all things in Christ
Who empowers me [I am ready for anything and equal

113

to anything through Him Who infuses inner strength into
me; I am self-sufficient in Christ's sufficiency].

Philippians 4:13 (AMP)

As the fast was about to end, I began to anticipate great
results. The Lord did not disappoint me. Each time I had
done a three-day fast I noticed a difference in me, and now
this was a week-long fast. It was then that I realized God
was birthing a completely new person. The Lord began to
heal the heaviness of my past. Layers of hurt were peeling
away with each fast. Sins that had manifested as fits of anger,
slander and gossip, and a judgmental spirit began to fall by
the wayside. God was setting me free with each fast.

I could not see the whole picture; I kept thinking this was
just all about "obedience" to Him. Perhaps this was partially
true. I believe God was testing me to see how much I desired
Him. There were (and still are) times during my fasting when
I cried out to Him and said, "Lord I want you more than
food." Indeed, now I am actually hungry for Him! I want
His anointing, and know that it comes through seeking after
Him. When people see me, I want people to see a living, vital
relationship with the Lord. I want my ministry to be "real."
Through fasting I became desperate for Him, and I developed
a stronger desire to be used by the Lord. I pled with Him to
give me more of Him! He became my greatest desire.

This was an incredible journey. I know it sounds bizarre,
but through the seeking and suffering in fasting, the Lord
worked a true miracle in me. This discipline over food also
helped in other areas of weakness. My faith became stronger,
and during my time of fasting I learned who He really is.

It is beyond description how real God and His Word have
become to me through this discipline. In addition, I have
prayed to receive a spirit of wisdom and revelation as spoken
about in Ephesians, Chapter 1. I believe He is answering this

prayer a little at a time. I have such clarity in the Word now, as though a light in my head suddenly came on. I finally understand his love for others and me. I am not saying I have all knowledge, but I do have a much deeper understanding. It was as though all the knowledge I had learned went from my head into my heart. Once that happened, I was able to apply it to my everyday life.

The change in me became so evident that even my family noticed. God in His grace gave me confirmation of the work. A friend of mine, Carrie, told me she had a discussion with her daughter Taylor about my family.

She said that Taylor and Amanda (my daughter) were eating lunch together. Amanda mentioned to Taylor how glad she was that I had quit my job. Amanda said, "I am glad my mother is home this year; there has been such a change in her since she has been studying the Word and fasting." My daughter noticed!

Ladies, do you realize the true miracle that has occurred in me? When your own children comment on the change, then you know there is real change! It is real, because He is real!

Even my prayer life began to transform as I fasted. I began to pray differently; I felt moved to ask God, "Let me see others as You see them." How astonishing! He answered that prayer immediately! I was becoming a "doer of the Word" and not just a hearer only. Now that healing had come to my life, God began to use me in many areas. Opportunities for ministry opened up. I began to speak at conferences, which is my heart's desire. Doors opened for my family to volunteer at a facility for high-risk teens. As we volunteered with these kids, it made me realize how much I had in common with them. It became apparent to me that there is such a need in hurting people for hope. I pray my life gives them a reason to hope, and that is my main motivation for writing this book. Through the power of Jesus Christ, I have been victorious over a childhood very similar to theirs, one that was full of rejection. I want to encourage them that Jesus can do the same thing for them that He did for me.

I have heard many gut wrenching stories of how teens end up at this particular facility. The majority of them are "thrown away" by our society. To God, however, they are broken teens He desires to restore and build up. Each one of these teens has value, and to help facilitate their worth is the mission of our visits.

The typical teens in this place come from an environment of substance or sexual abuse, and they have been taken out of their home. The next phase of their lives has usually been the foster care system. Within that system, many of them were again physically and sexually abused. This place is probably the last resort before juvenile hall or a psychiatric hospital. Eventually some of the kids may return home, depending on the circumstances.

One of my family's favorite cabins to visit is the cabin for the mentally handicapped. These teens are not severe by any means; they usually just have learning disabilities, often resulting from being born with fetal alcohol syndrome, a birth defect caused by a mother drinking an excessive amount of alcohol during pregnancy. My family and I always enjoy the time we share with these special-needs children. We teach a Bible lesson, do a craft, and sometimes my children sing songs to them. When we visit we usually take a treat, maybe popsicles or a drink. This is special to these kids. They love it when we come; we can see it in their faces! We talk with them and tell them how much the Lord loves them, and that we do too. Ministering like this has changed my own children. My children will even verbalize how grateful they are for their family and home. My children (ages fifteen, thirteen, and eleven) have all ministered to these wounded teens. It is an awesome experience to see your own kids reach out to others. Perhaps you can see that ministry is easier than you think! It just takes a little time and a few hugs, but it will change your heart forever. The most awesome thing is that my pain from the past has been turned around for good, and God is glorified in the process!

Ladies, when God first called me to fast, I could never imagine that my own healing would come from obedience to this discipline. It took me years to acquire those layers of hurt and pain, but with my fasting and seeking, the Lord peeled away many layers of these troubles in just a matter of months! He did such a deep, internal work in me that I still stand amazed! The new insight and understanding He gave me concerning His Word is something I will treasure forever! It truly is more precious than gold.

The most magnificent thing of all is that He has not stopped! He is continuing to do this work! Believe it or not, fasting can be a wonderful experience, but the Lord should lead it. I now look forward to fasting because of the results I receive. The blessings are immeasurable.

> ...so that your fasting will not be noticed by men,
> but by your Father who is in secret; and your Father
> who sees what is done in secret will reward you.

Matthew 6:18 (NASU)

Ladies, the Lord desires to reward you. Be obedient and you will reap beyond measure.

Please do not misunderstand; the methodology is not the key. It was not a certain formula or a specific number of fasting days that healed my wounded spirit. It was the Lord. Yes, there is power in this fasting, and it is tremendous! Nonetheless, God is always looking at our heart and testing our motives as we go before Him. He sees the real you. If you are going to fast to lose weight, or fast just to be "fasting," you are wasting your time! I did not impress Him with my fasting any more than I am trying to impress you.

I am sharing my experience. Do not try to copy my experience. This is not a boxed solution to your problems. Fasting is not a "work" that gains you extra favor; it does not earn your salvation. Remember, favor comes only through obedience, but grace (unmerited favor) cannot be earned.

> For by grace you have been saved through faith;
> and that not of yourselves, it is the gift of God;
> not as a result of works, so that no one may boast.
> For we are His workmanship, created in Christ Jesus
> for good works, which God prepared beforehand
> so that we would walk in them.

Ephesians 2:8-10 (NASU)

Please understand that fasting is about denying self and surrendering to Him, which allows God the freedom to go deeper in our lives. My yielding could only be learned through fasting, and considering my strong will, God knew that I needed a longer fast and more than one fast.

Do you want more of God? Is He calling you to fast? Honestly, I do not believe you can reach certain heights with God without fasting, praying, and giving of yourself (time and money). Remember, we are to imitate Christ. If Jesus himself fasted, prayed, and gave of Himself, why shouldn't we? This will expedite the hand of God to move in any situation.

Ask God if fasting would help you demolish any stronghold you may have. Maybe you too are struggling with anger, eating disorders, or even a habit you would like to break, such as smoking. I know God is able to help in any situation. Fasting could be the road He takes to heal those inner wounds. Ask Him; He will supply what you need. If it is a healing of the past or a broken heart, He has got you covered.

> And <u>my God</u> will meet all your needs
> according to his glorious riches in Christ Jesus.

> Philippians 4:19 (NIV)

Did you see how Paul personalized his relationship by saying "my God?" Make Him "your God" and ask Him to leave His thumbprint on every situation in your life. You will see His hand at work!

If you choose to fast, there are several practical things you can do to help increase your chances of success. Fasting brings temptation to eat, so I suggest that you plan your fast before you begin. Prepare meals for your family ahead of time, and watch how much food you eat within the few days before your fast begins. You need to eat lightly and go without caffeine a couple of days before your fast, so any headaches will not be quite as severe.

The first day of your fast will be the worst, and each day after that will get easier. The duration of your fast is between you and the Lord. I have also done a ten-day "Daniel Fast," and some day I would like to do a twenty-one-day "Daniel Fast." This fast is fashioned after Daniel's eating habits in the court of Nebuchadnezzer. As with Daniel, I ate nothing but fruit and vegetables and drank only water for the allotted time. Many people participate in this type of fast. After completing this fast, I felt so healthy. It was a tremendous time with the Lord. The story of Daniel and Hananiah, Mishael, and Azariah (also known as Shadrach, Meshach, and Abednego) is found in Daniel 1:12-16 (NIV):

> "Please test your servants for ten days: Give
> us nothing but vegetables to eat and water to drink.
> Then compare our appearance with that of the young
> men who eat the royal food, and treat your servants in

accordance with what you see." So he agreed to this
and tested them for ten days.

At the end of the ten days they looked healthier
and better nourished than any of the young men
who ate the royal food. So the guard took away
their choice food and the wine they were to drink
and gave them vegetables instead.

Daniel 1:12-16 (NIV)

Not only does fasting produce spiritual benefits, but health benefits as well. It will expunge toxins, rest the digestive system, and some believe it will accomplish the repair of vital organs. Whatever God requests of you, you know it will never harm you. So if the Lord is calling you to a fast, do it without hesitation. The rewards will be boundless. Trust Him. He will never let you down.

When I fast, I do not let anyone know what I am doing. My fasting time is between the Lord and me only. I will not tell you about these intimate times with the Lord, for I did not write this to boast. All I want is for people to be healed and walk closer to the Lord. I pray this discussion on fasting helps sets you free from the prison of generational sins.

If the Lord is asking you to fast, then please be cognizant of Him. He only desires the finest for you. If you can grasp that concept, obeying becomes a lot easier. Ponder the next verse, and you will have a greater desire to do the Lord's will in your life. Ladies, obedience is the key to being a successful Christian!

Does the LORD delight in
burnt offerings and sacrifices as much as in obeying

the voice of the LORD? To obey is better than sacrifice,
And to heed is better than the fat of rams.

1 Samuel 15: 22 (NIV)

CHAPTER NINE

She's Got Personality!

My frame was not hidden from You when I was being
formed in secret [and] intricately and curiously wrought
[as if embroidered with various colors] in the depths of the
earth [a region of darkness and mystery].

Your eyes saw my unformed substance,
and in Your book all the days [of my life]
were written before ever they took shape,
when as yet there was none of them.

How precious and weighty also are Your thoughts to me,
O God! How vast is the sum of them!

Psalm 139:15-17 (AMP)

Have you ever thought about your personality? I have
mine. I have wondered why I am such a gregarious
person and why some of my children are not. Among my
four children, two are very shy and the other two are very
outgoing, but they become uncomfortable in a crowd. How
different we are, and yet we are all in the same family.

How do you feel about your personality? I have mixed feelings about mine. I am a classic extrovert; I am not afraid to walk up to a stranger and ask a question. I will smile and say hello to any stranger on an elevator. I love to socialize! Being in a large gathering amongst many people is to me, great fun! I am truly a people person, and I believe that if this is the way God made me, then He must have a purpose for this personality He gave me, right?

However, at times with this personality, I can appear domineering. I have been known to speak my mind without being aware that it offended someone. It seemed I was only making my opinion known. When this occurred, I would get frustrated with myself, and there have been many times I have struggled with this aspect of my personality. I asked God, "Why did You give me this personality? What am I to do with my bluntness? How can I use it for good?" Honestly, I have even felt as though I was stuck with a curse! What made matters worse is that when I was feeling most sorry for myself about this, I would always seem to run into "Ms. Sweet Christian Woman." You know the one with the perfect "meek and quiet spirit." Of course, I then wonder, *What is wrong with me, and why can't I be like her?*

Have you ever had thoughts such as this? These questions bothered me for years. Why did I always feel compelled to speak out? Was there something wrong with me? He did heal me from many things. But after the healing, I was still left with a bold personality.

Then finally the answer came as I studied God's Word. After a few months of intense study, I was able to comprehend that it was a "personality gift" and not a "personality curse." It was not my personality that was the problem, but instead there was a lack of wisdom in my behavior!

A good definition of wisdom can be found in the book of James.

But the wisdom from above is first of all
pure (undefiled); then it is peace-loving, courteous
(considerate, gentle). [It is willing to] yield
to reason, full of compassion and good fruits;
it is wholehearted and straightforward, impartial and
unfeigned (free from doubts, wavering, and insincerity).

James 3:17 (AMP)

The Word tells us to pray for wisdom and it will be given to us. It is not always *what* we say, but *how and when we say it* that reflects wisdom. And quite often wisdom is expressed by not saying anything at all.

As I studied more, I also recognized that many of my "bold" actions were not grounded in love. God gave me this personality for a purpose, but it wasn't to rip people up or make them feel unworthy. He gave me this personality to boldly speak His Word in truth, but while doing that, He also wants me to be rooted and established in love. I found this out by studying Ephesians.

Rather, let our lives lovingly express
truth [in all things, speaking truly, dealing truly,
living truly]. Enfolded in love, let us grow up in every
way and in all things into Him Who is the Head,
[even] Christ (the Messiah, the Anointed one).

Ephesians 4:15 (AMP)

Once I grasped the love of the Lord, then I was able to comprehend better who I was in Christ. Christ's dying became a reality! I finally understood that Christ loved me so much that He wanted to use me to help others. This revelation affected me like never before. He had given me this personality to build others up and not to tear them down. My boldness was to be used to share His Word in love. As I had stated before, my actions had not always been in love. When I finally caught on to this knowledge, I immediately obeyed and the results were dramatic.

Have you ever struggled with facets of your personality? What are your strengths and weaknesses? Would you like to see a change in your personality? Are you frustrated, as I was? If so, all I can say to you is that God loves variety, and whatever personality He gave you — whether shy, outgoing, witty, or serious — He wants to reveal His glory in who you are *through* that personality. The only thing you may need is a little correction and training, as I did.

Obedience to the Word became a priority to me. Once this happened, God started to clean up many areas of my life. He began to speak gently to me about a "controlling" element within my personality. During my turbulent childhood, the adults in my life could not be trusted, and so I had become adamant about not letting anyone direct my path. Therefore, controlling my environment became a driving force in my life. Because of my past, I had formed some bad habits based on demanding my way. However, God in His sovereignty would not let me stay in this awful state. He worked that junk right out of me.

As God began to heal my wounded spirit, I knew it was time to relinquish this need for control. I assumed this was going to be a difficult task, because to me, control was a "sacred cow." It was very frightening for me to hand it over. What would happen to me? Could I trust anyone else with that control? Still, I knew I needed to go to the next step with Him. Surprisingly, it was easier than I thought. It did not happen over night, of course, but was (and still is) an on-going process. At the time, the Lord revealed that my dominant personality was putting stress on my relationships and on me personally. I was carrying burdens I was not meant to carry. It is difficult for me to explain how much better my everyday life became, but it certainly was much more peaceful. I found it easier to live the Word daily.

Once God dealt with me to turn over "control" to Him, I could see the next step. God dealt with me on what it meant to be a true helpmate to my husband Randy! I realized that my job is to make him the best man he can be, just as his job is to make me the best woman I can be! We are partners in this marriage. Let me share with you some of the insight God used to help me be a better partner.

Randy and I are wired completely differently in how we manage daily tasks. Randy is more of a "Type B" personality. He rarely gets upset. He is very spontaneous. He is just easy-going and fun to be around! On the other hand, my personality tends to lean more towards being a "Type A" than a "Type B." I like to plan my day. In fact, I like to set daily goals and mark off those goals as I meet them.

On top of these personality differences, Randy has ADHD (Attention Deficit Hyperactive Disorder). What this means for Randy is that he has trouble keeping track of things! He has to write himself notes, and his desk and steering wheel serve as his bulletin boards with notes all over them, helping him get through his day. His mind is racing all the time! People who have been diagnosed with this disorder are usually very intelligent and creative, and I would say that also defines Randy. All of this helps him to be very good at his profession. His clients love him and he loves them. He prays for His clients and seeks God's wisdom in his job. Randy loves his job, but sometimes the overly detailed work gives him trouble. If Randy is distracted from the task at hand, he may even forget what his previous task was! He also struggles with organization, yet with the grace of God and a great staff at his work, he is able to get a lot done in a day. We both have achieved a lot of balance by understanding that God put us together to help one another.

This happy balance was not always the case in his work and in our marriage. I probably was frustrated with him ten percent of the time. I would ask him to pick up something from the store and of course, he would forget. Then I would express my aggravation with him verbally. I was so used to speaking my mind, even with Randy. My words pierced like a knife without my realizing it. Randy felt disparaged. I should have realized that speaking negatively does not accomplish anything but producing negativity! My "chewing out" behavior did not help me either. After I was finished, I always felt terrible, so no one was winning this battle (except Satan, of course). This behavior went on far too long.

Learning to work within our different personalities was a challenge but was not an impossibility. I began to understand that part of my job as a wife was to help Randy manage his ADHD. I was to be an encourager, not a discourager. Again, as I abided in love and in the Word, the stresses in my life began to subside.

Now I call Randy and ask him to write things down. I ask him to repeat them back to me. Maybe on his way home, I call him and ask him if he has his note. We are in this marriage for life, and my job is to help him get through his day, just like how he does for me when he comes home and helps around the house. I want him to be successful in everything he does. Having this attitude has improved our marriage immensely! I can honestly say Randy and I are more in love now than we have ever been before!

Thank God, I have come to a place in my Christian walk that I care more about obeying Him than I do saving my pride. I want to be a good wife. The Lord is continuing to turn the light on. At present, He is helping me to see Randy from a new perspective and to treat him with the respect he deserves. I will be honest here: I had been so busy raising our children and working that I let those activities consume me. I was guilty of giving Randy what little was left over at the end of the day. The Lord has shown me that soon my children will be raised, but my relationship with Randy will continue. It is the most important relationship I have outside of my relationship with the Lord. I now protect and cherish my time with Randy. I am now living the life I once dreamed of. There is nothing healthier for our children than to see their mom and dad truly love one another. It also gives them that security I so desired as a child. Isn't it remarkable what Jesus will do once you surrender to His authority and let Him take control of your life? Every area of your life falls into sync in an amazing way.

Because of Jesus Christ and His work in me through His Word, I now understand that God has given me a bold, "Type A" personality for a reason, and that is to preach the Gospel. I am not shy about speaking the truth! It is my passion, because it is the only hope for this world. The process He chose to heal me has shown me firsthand the power of His Word! It really does set people free! It gives life! It gives wisdom! My life has drastically changed since I applied these principals to my everyday living. The Word of God works! It is not a rulebook, but instead is an adventurous treasure map that will guide your every step. It will show you how to live successfully in every facet of life. It is not just about living an average "good" life, but rather an extraordinary, adventurous life with God!

God is an amazing sculptor, able to take anyone's "garbage" and recycle it. He does not waste one moment of our lives. He is in the business of sculpting us into the image of His son, making each of us His masterpiece! I will take His image over mine any day; wouldn't you?

And we know that in all things God works
for the good of those who love him,
who have been called according to his purpose.

Rom 8:28-29 (NIV)

CHAPTER TEN

On My Way Out!

─◦◦◦─

My son, if you accept my words and store up my
commands within you, turning your ear to wisdom and
applying your heart to understanding, and if you call out
for insight and cry aloud for understanding, and if you look
for it as for silver and search for it as for hidden treasure,
then you will understand the fear of the LORD and find the
knowledge of God. For the LORD gives wisdom, and from
his mouth come knowledge and understanding. He holds
victory in store for the upright; he is a shield to those whose
walk is blameless, for he guards the course of the just and
protects the way of his faithful ones.
Then you will understand what is right and just and fair
— every good path. For wisdom will enter your heart, and
knowledge will be pleasant to your soul. Discretion will
protect you, and understanding will guard you.
Wisdom will save you from the ways of wicked men, from
men whose words are perverse, who leave the straight paths
to walk in dark ways.

Proverbs 2:1-13 (NIV)

When we moved to the new community to be closer to
our children's school, I was asked by many to lead a

Bible study, but I just was not ready. Another neighbor said she would lead it but asked if we could have it at my house. Of course, I agreed. She began a study and it was very good, but in the middle of the study some family problems arose, and soon she felt as though the Lord wanted her to lay it down. Guess who she asked to fill her absence? Correct! The next thing I knew, I was leading the Bible study, ready or not! I was a little apprehensive, but before I knew it, I had fallen in love with the Word of God.

When the women came to my house to study and discuss God's Word, it became my favorite time of the week. It kept me accountable to the Word and whetted my appetite for more. I desired a closer walk. It is so true that the more you are in the Word, the more you will desire it! The first year we did the Bible study there were eight women who attended. The second year it began to grow and I do mean grow! There were twenty women now in this neighborhood study! Can you believe the Lord entrusted me to lead a study with twenty women in attendance? I cannot!

These Bible studies were developing me into a more mature Christian. It was in leading the Bible study that I noticed how some of my past prejudices and opinions had derived from incorrect teaching. The power in the Word is amazing! I became very disciplined in the Word and studied faithfully. I believe this was "phase one" of the healing process for my bitter spirit. The Word of God is so powerful. It really can heal a broken heart, if you believe. I am grateful for the words of Isaiah, the prophet:

So shall My word be that goes forth out of My
mouth: it shall not return to Me void [without producing
any effect, useless], but it shall accomplish that which

I please and purpose, and it shall prosper in the thing
for which I sent it.

Isaiah 55:11 (AMP)

Even though my attitude was marred with little calluses, the Lord allowed me to continue teaching that Bible study for two years. I am so thankful, because I certainly was not "perfect," but I benefited greatly, and there was a tremendous change in my life after each study we completed. Little did I know that He was preparing me for the next phase of my healing process.

In the year 2000, I was asked to teach high school social studies in a Christian high school. What a thrill! I love history and politics! I began to study and tried to learn the subject. This required a lot of hard work on my part, since I had graduated from college ten years prior and had been very busy with raising my four children. Obviously, I did not keep up with history unless it was something on *Barney* or *Sesame Street*!

Soon I was guiding a Bible study every Tuesday afternoon, and teaching high school social studies every morning! I was really too busy, yet I was compelled to lead that Bible study for the remainder of the school year. I am so glad that I did. It pushed me into studying the Word, even though I felt swamped with all of the teaching preparation. The truth was that I needed that study just as much as the other women did. Since I worked with teenagers, I needed the Word even more to survive.

Some of the students were patient with me and others were not, and a couple of students were downright disrespectful. If I had been in this situation prior to the Bible study, I probably would have exploded and ripped their little heads clean off their bodies! (I don't think that would have gone over very well in a Christian school, do you?) Because of the work the Lord had performed in my heart, I realized that hurting people hurt people. Having that knowledge gave me insight as to why some of these students were so cruel. I lost my temper a couple of times, but I was much more controlled than in the past. God's work in me was still in the developmental stage, but He was working on changes for the better.

During my years of teaching God began showing me that instead of making judgments about certain students, I should be praying for them. Many of these kids came from homes that were in disarray. He began to show me their pain. A few students would share what was going on at home. When the kids started to act out their appalling behavior, I began to see their wounded hearts instead of getting upset. I understood that they were reacting to their hurtful situation, just as I had once done.

Aren't you glad that God sees and understands the root of our bad behavior? Of course He loves us too much to let us stay there, but He is patient. His patience was revealed to me in deeper ways through teaching at this school. It became the second phase to my healing; it opened my eyes to how many people are hurting "out there." Here I was teaching in a Christian school, with students supposedly from "good" homes and Christian parents. How wrong I was to think they escaped the pain of family strife. I had one student in particular who was very bright but would not put any effort into his work. His parents were divorced, and he rarely saw his mom. He spoke so highly of her. One day he looked at me, with all of eighteen years of experience, and asked me directly, "Mrs. Sauer, will you be my mom?" Right then I knew exactly what he was feeling. He was longing for what I had longed for at his age. My heart ripped in two.

I replied, "Of course I will be your mom." It was after this I realized these kids were dealing with the same problems as non-Christian kids. Oh, how I desire that we adults realize that every choice we make affects everyone around us — especially our children.

In the school where I taught, most of the high school teachers had been teaching together for many years. They had developed their cliques over time, and I was just the "new pup." I was scared to death; I did not know squat about teaching. It had been years since I had graduated from college. One thing I found out quickly: college teaches the "philosophy of teaching," but not the practicalities of how it is done. Teaching is a skill that is learned through trial and error.

These seasoned teachers were very serious about teaching, and here I was being quite jovial and trying to make the best out of a difficult situation. We did not mix very well. I do not believe it was intentional, but they more or less ostracized me. They were overwhelmed with all their own work and did not have time to mentor or even encourage me. I can remember walking down the hall and looking straight into one of the cliques, greeting them with a smile and a big "hello" and getting only silence as a response. This happened more than once. If someone did speak, it was out of politeness. These teachers' actions — however unintentional — sliced deeply into my self-esteem. It seemed that since I was only a "part-time" employee, they felt it was useless for them to take me under their wing and befriend me. It also did not help that my room was located on the other side of the building and our paths rarely crossed. I was so isolated! It affected me so deeply that I went home crying about it a few times. In all fairness, a couple of the teachers made an effort to speak to me in passing, and I did very much appreciate it. Even though this was all so upsetting to me at the time, I now realize that God was doing a work in me that was preparing me for ministry. Instead of wallowing in my self-pity or committing character assassination on these teachers (as I would have done in the past), I began to take my complaints to the Lord. I told Him how much these individuals hurt me! You know what the Lord began to do? He began to deal with my heart, and He gave me insight into why some people behave in hurtful ways.

He began to show me several things. First, He began to soften my heart. Then He had me look at these individuals from a new perspective. While I was crying out about *my* pain, He spoke to me about *their* pain! He told me not to take it personally, but instead to pray for them. He said, "These people are part of my church, and the church is too busy to let Me heal them." He showed me that their lack of friendliness had little to do with me and more to do with how they were feeling about themselves. They, too, do not realize who they are in Christ. The Lord knows my heart and the compassion I have for the insecure. It is hard to judge and get offended at people when you know they are hurting.

Now I realize that these individuals are struggling. How I would love to share with them what God could do in their lives. If given the chance, I would tell them that God loves them and has great plans for them. I pray they catch His fresh vision for their lives so they can receive the wonderful future He has for them. There is great freedom in Christ!

The fourth year I was at this school, God sent me on a mission trip to Mexico with the high school. Here I was, forty years old and going on my first mission trip! All Christians should go on a mission trip if they are financially able to do so. I was a sponsor with the school and helped chaperone thirty-some teens. I had to share a room with twenty high school girls and two other sponsors. We slept in bunk beds, took fast showers, ate three meals a day, and had a great time ministering everywhere we went! We went on the streets, performed dramas, and prayed for the people. We hugged the people and witnessed about Jesus. People gathered around, waiting for the Americans to pray for them. It was a wonderful time! God opened my heart and filled it with His love for these people. While in Mexico, I was asked to speak at a drug rehabilitation facility. I said yes without hesitation. I shared a little of my own story and my past drug activity. I told them I understood their despair, and I gave them the Word to comfort them. After I finished, my interpreter looked at me and said, "You are a preacher!" In that moment, I suddenly realized that this is the business God wanted me in, the "people" business. He opened my eyes to the world full of lost souls and gave me such a desire to lead them to Christ! Beloved, I stepped out of my comfort zone and received a calling from God! This was not just a learning experience, but it was also a spiritual high. Who needs drugs when you have the Holy Spirit?

Now I want everyone to have this same revelation. If you are out shopping and you run into someone you know who takes no notice of you or does not even speak, do not get angry. Pray for them instead. Do not take it personally. The first idea that may pop into your mind is, "What a snob!" or "Who do they think they are? I can't believe I just saw her at the game and she acted like we were friends, and now she won't even speak to me!" Look beyond your offense and realize they may be struggling with themselves. I promise you if you think compassionately and pray for people, you will be set free. If you want to be like Christ, you have to get over yourself! Get "yourself" off your mind, and see people around you as Christ sees them. If you see people as Christ sees them, you become an empathetic Christian, and isn't that the way to truly be Christ-like?

The word "empathetic" comes from the word empathy, which means to understand, as in a vicarious situation, "to be sensitive." This is a difficult concept to grasp, but I know that you want to be more like Christ. This is where you have to die to your flesh. Dying to your flesh is probably the most complicated process you will do as a Christian. I cannot say it enough: anytime you step out of your comfort zone and go beyond yourself, you will be blessed beyond measure.

Peace will come upon you that surpasses all understanding. It is awesome!

As you can see, the way God has worked in my life in preparing me for the ministry has been in phases. First, He let me lead a Bible study and thereby watered me with His Word; then, He revealed to me just how many of us are walking around wounded, both teachers and students! Most are not living the Christian life in full measure, even those who work in churches and Christian schools. People are not realizing what He is capable of doing.

He not only binds up the broken-hearted, but He can actually create a new heart.

> I will give you a new heart and put a new spirit in
> you; I will remove from you your heart of stone and
> give you a heart of flesh.
>
> Ezekiel 36:26-27 (NIV)

Beloved, He is the only one who can take our wounded hearts and make them new. He will take all the ashes of a life and turn them into diamonds. I am so different now that I even like myself! Now I understand what He means when He states, "Love others as you love yourself." Rather than making you self-centered, loving yourself the way He loves you actually motivates you to love others.

Do you need Him to fix your situation? If you are ready to let Him, He is able. I am living proof of His power. I know what He did with my wounded spirit!

God does not have favorites. What He does for one, He will do for another. That includes you!

34 Then Peter began to speak: "I now realize how true it is
that God does not show favoritism
Acts 10:34 (NIV)

CHAPTER ELEVEN

Freedom

—⊙⁂⊸—

Sing, O Daughter of Zion;
shout aloud, O Israel!
Be glad and rejoice with all your heart,
O Daughter of Jerusalem!
The LORD has taken away your punishment,
he has turned back your enemy.
The LORD, the King of Israel, is with you;
never again will you fear any harm.
On that day they will say to Jerusalem,
"Do not fear, O Zion;
do not let your hands hang limp.
The LORD your God is with you,
he is mighty to save.
He will take great delight in you,
he will quiet you with his love,
he will rejoice over you with singing."

The sorrows for the appointed feasts
I will remove from you;
they are a burden and a reproach to you.
At that time I will deal
with all who oppressed you.

Zephaniah 3:19 (NIV)

These verses were written for you. They are for everyone who wants to take hold of them. These verses promise victory. If you are in bondage, then let me tell you, help is on the way!

God has healed me from the lingering effects of neglect, rejection, and abandonment. I became a new person in mid-life. It was like being born all over again, except with a much clearer understanding of who He is.

Ladies, everyone comes with their own baggage from the past. Acknowledging this is no different from going to the doctor and revealing your family medical history. The doctor wants to know if there is any heart disease or diabetes, because he knows it affects your health today. In the same way, you can also be carrying some of your parents' spiritual and emotional baggage--issues they never dealt with that affect your own spiritual and emotional health today. Christ wants you to recognize this baggage, ask for healing, and be able to move on with His purposes for your life.

It really is possible to soar so high in your flight with Jesus
that the past is thrown in the "depths of the sea"
as you make your trip.

He will again have compassion on us; He will
subdue and tread underfoot our iniquities. You will cast all
our sins into the depths of the sea
Micah 7:19 (AMP)

It all has to do with your heart. All He requires is that you yield to Him. It is a sad thing that many of us hold onto our "baggage" for dear life, as if we were going through La Guardia Airport in New York! Why do we do this? I guess many hold on to their "baggage" because it is familiar. They are scared of the unknown. It is also intimidating to admit that we are not perfect, and that everything might not be as great about our life as we thought. But I say, go ahead, admit it, and get rid of it! Look inward, get over it, and let it go!

Are you ready for a change? The first step to change is admitting there is a problem. If you are ready to make changes in your life, tell God that you know something is not right, and ask Him to reveal the problem. There might be a spirit of unforgiveness, bitterness, anger, or some other bondage. Ask Him how to deal with it. He will begin to show you!

He revealed to me that the root of my problem was unforgiveness. He made me aware that all the resentment I held in my heart was affecting me, not the ones I was angry with. It was making me hard and bitter. As I began to repent, God led me to a book called *The Bondage Breaker.* In this book, Neil T. Anderson suggests that the reader write down the names of everyone that he or she may have unforgiveness toward. I did this exercise and admitted my unforgiveness to the Lord. Then the Lord led me to read 1 John 1:9.

If we [freely] admit that we have sinned and confess
our sins, He is faithful and just (true to His own nature and
promises) and will forgive our sins
[dismiss our lawlessness]
and [continuously] cleanse us from all unrighteousness
[everything not in conformity to His will in purpose,
thought, and action].

1 John 1:9 (AMP)

Once I admitted my unforgiveness was sin and let God search my heart, He revealed to me how much resentment I carried. Ladies, I am ashamed to say that this list consisted of more than just my mother and father. I had to make a cognitive decision to forgive all these people! Then, I prayed over each person and asked God to bless him or her. In order to forgive, I had to say audibly, with each person's name, "I choose to forgive my mother; I choose to forgive my father," and so on. Remember what God tells us about the power of our words. I did not want to "eat" bitterness anymore. I wanted to eat sweet tasting fruit!

21 The tongue has the power of life and death ,
and those who love it will eat its fruit.
Prov 18:21 (NIV)

For out of the **overflow of the heart**
the mouth speaks. The good man brings good
things out of the good stored up in him,
and the evil man brings evil things out
of the evil stored up in him.

Matthew 12:34-35 (NIV)

I knew I needed a heart change, so my words had to reflect the direction of my new heart. Did I feel forgiveness as soon as I did this? The answer is no. However, I knew if I obeyed God, my feelings would follow and these bondages would no longer have a hold on me. I had to fight the attacks of the devil in my thought life. When he threw negative thoughts at me, I had to take them captive. Paul tells us how to fight this fight in his second epistle to the Corinthian church:

For the weapons of our warfare are not physical
[weapons of flesh and blood], but they are mighty
before God for the overthrow
and destruction of strongholds,
[Inasmuch as we] refute arguments and theories
and reasonings and every proud and lofty thing that
sets itself up against the [true] knowledge of God; and

we lead every thought and purpose away captive into the obedience of Christ (the Messiah, the Anointed one).

2 Corinthians 10:4-5 (AMP)

Ladies, my unforgiveness, bitterness, and anger were strongholds. I wanted these generational sins to stop with me, and I was determined. I was not going to live in my prison anymore. This junk was **not** going to be carried on into the next generation. In order to be certain of this, I had to change my thinking. To live this Christian life victoriously and change the future for my own children required putting more of the Word in my heart and mind, and less of the world.

Beyond confessing forgiveness, in his book, *The Bondage Breaker*, Neil T. Anderson also suggests that to accelerate the healing process, one needs to write a letter to each person he or she needs to forgive, whether the letters are actually mailed or not.

I did as the author suggested for each person who had hurt me. I stated how I forgave him or her for the past, and I asked each person on my list to forgive me, too, for holding on to my resentment. As stated, such a letter does not always need to be sent. Possibly the letter cannot be sent, as in the case of my deceased parents. If you do this, you must pray and ask God if you should send this type of letter or not. Do your best to obey the Lord. Everything the Lord required of me previous had worked, so again I obeyed. After the letters were written and read aloud, I experienced such a release. Years of frustration and pain dissolved in a moment of forgiveness.

Forgiveness is the essence of Christianity. It is the most powerful ingredient of life we have as humans. Forgiveness is the element that can make a person whole again. Christ made me whole. Only after He put me on a regular fasting schedule did the Lord reveal to me the hidden unforgiveness in my heart. It would have been impossible for me to go into ministry unless I dealt with this unforgiveness.

I am so pleased that our Lord looks beyond our faults and sees what we can be once He is Lord of our weaknesses. Even in dealing with all my mistakes as a Christian, God never treated me with anger — only mercy. His graciousness toward me helped me understand the importance of forgiveness.

To deepen my understanding of this, He took me to the Word. I realized forgiveness was actually mandatory when I read this:

> For if you forgive people their
> trespasses [their reckless and willful sins, leaving
> them, letting them go, and giving up resentment],
> your heavenly Father will also forgive you. But if
> you do not forgive others their trespasses [their reckless
> and willful sins, leaving them, letting them go,
> and giving up resentment], neither will your
> Father forgive you your trespasses.

Matthew 6:14-15 (AMP)

That passage of Scripture made my blood run cold. Suddenly I realized that I did not have a choice. I *must* forgive! This Scripture was truly a lifesaver for me. I finally understood that my unforgiveness was hindering me from going forward. In fact, God's desire for His people is that we leave the past behind and move on!

> 18 "Forget the former things;
> do not dwell on the past.
> 19 See, I am doing a new thing!
> Now it springs up; do you not perceive it?

I am making a way in the desert
and streams in the wasteland.
Isa 43:18-19 (NIV)

The problem is we are not dealing with it and moving on. We have so much pride within the church, and pride is such an enemy! Pride only squelches growth. It is deceiving. Many choose to live in their mire rather than be set free. Many are living below their potential in Christ and do not even realize it. Ladies, you know the "King of kings and Lord of lords!" Sadly, when you mention that Jesus can heal people's wounds, they often do not even understand that they are wounded because of pride and unbelief. I have talked to many people who live in denial; they do not want to "face the music," and they make statements such as, "Christ did it all for me at Calvary," or "My past does not affect me since I accepted Christ." Honey, if you have not dealt with your past, then it is still affecting you. Yes, Christ did save you and me through Calvary, but the Word tells us that there is also a process called sanctification. We must work out our salvation with fear and trembling!

Therefore, my dear friends, as you have
always obeyed — not only in my presence, but now
much more in my absence — continue to work out
your salvation with fear and trembling, for it is
**God who works in you to will and to act according
to his good purpose.**

Philippians 2:12-13 (NIV)

God will do all the work, but we have to surrender to Him. We have to die to self. The fundamental nature of our flesh is to lead us into some sort of bondage, and this bondage has to be worked out of us. This is precisely why Christ came; He came to set us free from our own destructive ways.

Comprehending just how much God loves people was another eye-opener for me. I have been a Christian for over eighteen years now, and finally, I have gotten the revelation that Jesus wants me to share the love He shows me with others. I now understand that Christ saved me, I can trust Him, and I do not need to worry about myself anymore. I am free to be concerned for others, to be about "my Father's business," and that means the people business.

8 Let no debt remain outstanding, except the continuing debt to love one another, for he who loves his fellowman has fulfilled the law. 9 The commandments, "Do not commit adultery," "Do not murder," "Do not steal," "Do not covet," and whatever other commandment there may be, are summed up in this one rule: "Love your neighbor as yourself."   10 Love does no harm to its neighbor. Therefore love is the fulfillment of the law.
Rom 13:8-10 (NIV)

Last summer my husband had a business meeting in Washington, D.C. While Randy was downstairs in a conference, I spent most of my time in the room, yet a couple of times I went exploring the beautiful hotel we were staying in. The hotel was located right downtown, and it was decorated in the finest early colonial American style. The lobby was exquisite with marble floors, mahogany furniture, and a magnificent chandelier. Beloved, this was a fancy place! I decided to stroll down to the gym. As I walked down the gorgeous halls, I began to acknowledge people working in the hotel by speaking to them. They reacted with such surprise! Most other people were passing by, ignoring these individuals. I doubt that ignoring these precious people was deliberate; most people just have a tendency to be caught up in their own business. However, God had been speaking to me in this area and made it clear that He wanted me to pay attention to the people who served us by acknowledging and valuing them. Everyone has needs, and there are so many silent sufferers that something as simple as a kind word can be as extraordinary to a stranger as a touch from God.

For example, I needed to switch rooms because ours had a bad Internet connection. A bellhop came up with my new room key and helped me gather our luggage. As we were walking to my new room, I struck up a conversation. I asked him if he had a family. He told me yes, he had a wife and three children. We talked about family for about five minutes, and then he looked at me and remarked, "You are very nice." I was not trying to be nice. I truly was interested in him. The next day the maid knocked on our door to clean up the room. I complimented her on a job well done. She told me I was an "angel." Isn't that amazing? I became an "angel" to her just because of a compliment! Clearly, all people are hungry for love and respect, and Christ can use you and me to touch them in His name! God wants everyone to know he or she has great value to Him! Their place in society does not determine who they are in Christ!

One day I was watching Joyce Meyer's television program and she suggested that people should do a study on the word "love." She said, "Get a Bible concordance and look up every verse that has the word "love" in it." Ladies that is real insight! You will be amazed how this works! You must read all the verses repeatedly until it sinks in that God loves you deeply, and others, too. You are more than a conqueror when it comes to God's love! You are victorious. The Word tells us that nothing can come between us and the love of God. This concept needs to leave our heads and swell up in our hearts! Ponder it for a while.

Yet amid all these things we are more than
conquerors and gain a surpassing victory through
Him Who loved us. For I am persuaded beyond
doubt (am sure) that neither death nor life, nor angels
or principalities, nor things impending and threatening
nor things to come, nor powers, Nor height nor depth,
or anything else in all creation will be able to separate us
from the love of God which is in Christ Jesus our Lord.

Romans 8:37-39 (AMP)

Once you realize the love of the Lord for yourself and
others, you are able to walk in a new dimension of the Spirit.
Life really gets exciting. It becomes an escapade. When you
walk in the Spirit, you never know what might happen! You
may be thinking, "Right! That is exactly why I do not want
to "walk in the Spirit!" However, wait! If this is you, you are
missing out! There is nothing like the satisfaction of walking
with and pleasing the Lord. He has given me some amazing
adventures as I spread His love. The Spirit has led me to
take food over to a stranger's house (anonymously) with a
card that states, "I am praying for you," signed, "Someone
who loves Jesus." I have paid for strangers' groceries (this
is one of my favorites). I have given the church money and
directed it to a certain recipient, and the person never knew
where the money came from. Twice a month my entire
family gets in on this adventure as we go and show love to
broken teens at a facility nearby, and pray that God will heal
them as He did me.

The adventures with the Holy Spirit have taken me on
mission trips to Mexico and Haiti where I was blessed to
serve others and work like a dog! In Mexico I helped build
a canal, pulled weeds for a day, played with children in an
orphanage, and preached at a drug rehab center for women.
In January of 2006 I went to Haiti and taught on the book

of Ephesians at a women's conference. It was an amazing experience for me! If you had told me I would be involved in ministry even five years ago, I would have never believed you. Now I just want to be where God's heart is and where His hands and feet are needed. I want the things that break God's heart to break mine. I want to see the world changed by Christ. I know it is the truth and we can find hope in. So if you want to live in high exploration, get over yourself!

If *you* have failed you, I know that God will not. If your money fails you, know that God never runs out. Drugs and alcohol will leave you empty, but Jesus will fill you up. He loves us so much that He gave His life for us. He held nothing back. He will express His love for you in your everyday life if you let go of yourself and hold nothing back from Him.

Beloved, now that is the way to live! Life is excessively short for you to hold onto that old heavy "baggage." Get rid of it today! Be the first to say, "I'm sorry." Do not waste another moment on your pity. Get honest with God and tell Him how you feel and what you need. What happened to you as a child was not your fault and was not within your power to control, but what you do with today is! Ask for that healing, and then get ready to be thrust into an adventure.

In many ways I am glad I was rejected and abandoned, if I had not been, I would not know first hand of His goodness. Instead, I know He is real! I know Him personally as "Jehovah-Rapha," the healing God, the One who healed and delivered me.

Because of my yielding to the Lord, my children will reap the benefits far better than I ever dreamed possible. They no longer have a mother who throws raging fits or is bitter. They have a mother who is capable of love. I am very involved in their lives. I rarely miss a sporting event. I encourage them in everything they do. My children are good students and love school. We have been consistent in our discipline. My children know how special they are to me. Not only do I tell them often, but also I show them love and affection. The generational behaviors has been broken! The chains are off!

Because of the Word, they now have a mother who knows who she is in Christ. I have confidence of the love God has for me. Fear no longer rules me. If fear is consuming you, let these verses speak to you:

There is no fear in love [dread does not exist],
but full-grown (complete, perfect) love turns fear out of
doors and expels every trace of terror! For fear brings
with it the thought of punishment and [so] he who is afraid
has not reached the full maturity of love [is not yet grown
into love's complete perfection]. We love Him,
because He first loved us.

1 John 4:18-19 (AMP)

Those generational sins of my family are now broken through the blood of Jesus. I am out of the prison cell! Even my children have the revelation of that freedom. The letter on the next page is from my daughter, Ashley, given to me for Mother's Day.

Dear Mommy,

I did not have much money, but I wanted to give you something for Mother's Day, so I am writing you this letter. First of all, I want to tell you that you are amazing! I love you so much and I would not choose anyone else to be my mom. I hope to be just like you when I have kids of my own. You have always been the person I can trust the most, and I know I can go to you for anything in my life. I think this is really cool because I know you wouldn't of been able to say that about your parents. I can't even imagine what you went through during your childhood. It must have been very hard, but I am glad that God saved you. I am so thankful that I do not have to grow up even close to like you did. You have made my life awesome and I know that will continue. I also know that it is because you love me so much that you worked very hard to give me a different childhood than yours. I thank you from the bottom of my heart for that. You have protected me from many things and it is because you love me that you are strict at times. Even when we don't agree, you know the best for me. I am also so glad that we have a close relationship. Thank you so much for all that you have done for me. I love you with all my heart.

Happy Mother's Day!

Love,
Ashley

My healing is real and God has set me free! If it were not so, my daughter would not have written this letter. If I were still consumed with my own pain and problems, I would not be the parent God desires me to be. I would have missed the gratification in my spirit that comes from loving my family and helping others. I would not be able to go out and minister with confidence as I do now.

This must be why Satan loves to keep people wrapped up in their bondage. When you are in this bondage, you are so consumed with your own troubles that you cannot see a hurting world. You are incapable to be about your heavenly Father's business. You live in dread instead of hope. You become self-absorbed with your own feelings, worrying from day to day, with thoughts swirling around in your mind such as, *Oh God, how are you going to provide? What about me, Lord? Are you going to save so and so? Lord, help me get that new house, car, etc. Lord, what about this and that.* I am not saying it is wrong to pray about our needs, but if we are consumed with these types of prayers we are really in bondage to ourselves. Instead try praying for the opportunity to minister to others, and then you will see people delivered of substance abuse or other traps of bondage. He wants you to walk in faith. This is the secret to true happiness and a victorious life.

Because I am healed, I rejoice that the pain of the past is gone and no longer has a hold on me. The chains are off! I can look at my past and feel sorrow for my mother and father. I see that they lived in fear and disappointment. The devil consumed their every moment with his lies, and they lived them out. My mother and father never took the opportunity to get over themselves long enough to see Christ's glory. They did not have the teaching available to build their faith and help them realize what God is able to accomplish in a life truly given over to Him! Now when I think about them, anger is no longer there. Instead, my heart is full of compassion for them and for anyone else who is struggling in this area. A Christian without the understanding of the power of the Lord is a person in hopelessness. It is a sad existence. Now I understand the compassion the Lord had for my parents, just as He had for me when I was in my state of hopelessness. My sins were as dire as theirs were, except I am now living in victory because He has given me the "spirit of wisdom and revelation" of His Word.

Anyone can be set free from his or her prison. All you need is to believe and **apply** God's Word to your life. Believe it over your circumstances and be a doer of the Word. Take the Word seriously and live it out. This is what I did. Before He could use me in ministry, I had to discover this secret. It is not a hard concept, but it is something you must be determined to find. God performed a bona fide miracle in me. He will perform one for you, too! It will be remarkable. You will be free from that prison that you and others have built! Remember the story in Acts 16. Paul was in prison, but he chose to praise God. All of his chains were broken off. He was set free! Start praising God today, whatever your circumstance. You will see a miracle! He is longing to set you free. God is able! All you have to do is yield to Him!

Let us pray:

Lord, as I come before You, I first want to honor You and the power that is in Your name. You are so precious to me!

I ask that You reveal to me any sin in my life that I have received from prior generations, and I bind those sins in the name of Jesus. I pray this prayer over my children and myself. Alcoholism, divorce, mental illness, and incest must be gone in the name of Jesus. Your Word says that You show love to a thousand generations, and I

claim those promises for my children. Thank You, heavenly Father, that You have heard this prayer and that You will answer it. You are an Amazing God. Amen.

He upholds the cause of the oppressed and gives food to the hungry. **The LORD sets prisoners free**, the LORD gives sight to the blind, the LORD lifts up those who are bowed down, the LORD loves the righteous. The LORD watches over the alien and sustains the **fatherless** and the widow, but he frustrates the ways of the wicked. The LORD reigns forever, your God, O Zion, for all generations.
Praise the LORD.

Psalm 146:7-10 (NIV)

CONTACT INFORMATION

To contact Pamela Sauer,
or for more information about her ministry,

please email: pameladsauer@yahoo.com

Or, visit her website at:
www.pamsauer.org

Printed in the United States
57755LVS00002B/367-417

9 781600 341557